GET

≡ THE ≡

GUY

GET

= THE =

GUY

Learn Secrets of the Male Mind

to Find the Man You Want

and the Love You Deserve

MATTHEW HUSSEY

with Stephen Hussey

HARPER WAVE

An Imprint of HarperCollins*Publishers*

www.harperwave.com

3297753

HarperCollins books may be purchased for educational, business, or sales promotional use. For information, please e-mail the Special Markets Department at SPsales@ harpercollins.com.

FIRST EDITION

Library of Congress Cataloging-in-Publication Data
Hussey, Matthew, Relationship expert.
Get the guy : learn secrets of the male mind to find the man you want and the love you deserve / Matthew Hussey with Stephen Hussey.
p.   cm
ISBN 978-0-06-224174-0
1. Man-woman relationships—Psychological aspects. 2. Single women. 3. Single men—Psychology. 4. Dating (Social customs) I. Title.
HQ801.H955   2013
306.73—dc23
2013003845

13 14 15 16 17   OV/RRD   10 9 8 7 6 5 4 3 2 1

To the ultimate high-value woman,
my mum

This moment contains all moments.
—C. S. LEWIS

Contents

Introduction   xi

PART ONE: FIND THE GUY

1   Put the Odds in Your Favor   3
2   Being a Woman of High Value   19
3   Get a Social Life That Serves Your Love Life   30
4   The Mindset of the Chooser   46
5   The Traits of Desirable Women   58
6   The White Handkerchief Approach   67
7   From Great Conversation to First Date   84
8   The Joy of Text   94
9   A Word About Online Dating   99

PART TWO: GET THE GUY

10   The Ultimate Formula for Attraction   111
11   A Word About Insecurity   123
12   The Art of Creating the Great Date   130
13   The Sex Talk (Part I)   143
14   Stuck in the Friend Trap   153

15   Why Hasn't He Called?   168
16   Premature Obligation   180

PART THREE: KEEP THE GUY

17   How to Be the Woman of His Dreams   187
18   Is He Mr. Right?   198
19   What Guys Really Think About the C-Word   207
20   The Sex Talk (Part II)   216
21   If You Want Him to Commit   226
22   Love for Life   240

Acknowledgments   245

Introduction

Love is hard.

You love someone who doesn't love you back. You fall out of love with a guy you thought you'd love forever. Someone you love disappoints you. Or he leaves you. You fall for someone, hard, then never hear from him again. You've been burned, shut out, and heartbroken.

Even at the best of times, love can be traumatizing, like being punched in the gut. But isn't it amazing that although love sucks, we still want it in our lives? We patch up our hearts and go forth, hoping to find our real true love. Why? Why risk it all again? Because nothing feels as good as being in love. There is nothing better than lying in bed on a Sunday morning with someone who drives you wild. Nothing like the sound of your beloved's voice when he simply says, "Hello." There is no business opportunity, no promotion, no holiday, no amount of money that makes our hearts swell so.

Whatever your experiences with guys have been in the past, I know the odds are you will go out and try to find love again. This time, though, I'd like you to go back out with the tools and techniques that will help guarantee success in finding the man of your dreams.

===

So often I hear, where are all the good men? They're all around you! The problem is that you're not meeting them, simply because you haven't given yourself the opportunity to meet them. I'm not talking about meeting every player who's wagging his tongue at you from across the bar, but someone up to your standards, who's worth your time and attention.

Finding a guy isn't just about finding a guy. It's about living a life that engages you at every level and by extension creates opportunities for you to connect with many people. Some may well be guys you date, and one may be the man of your dreams. The real benefit to the techniques I teach is that you will raise the level at which you live your life. Women who live passionate lives are inherently sexy and attractive.

What I teach in this book is how you can be proactive in your love life without seeming desperate or easy, and how you can choose the man you want to meet but still get him to do the chasing. Most of all, I'll show you how to do this naturally, so that you never have to play games again.

═══

When I was just starting to notice girls, I used to wonder how other guys always seemed to be able to get the girl they wanted, while I somehow always ended up with whoever would have me. It drove me mad.

Even at a young age, I knew that there were rules of attraction that eluded me. The frustration I felt about my own lack of prowess spurred me to teach myself how to become acquainted with the girls to whom I was attracted, how to talk to them, how to attract them, and how to win them.

Over the years, I became more confident and successful. I believed I had tapped into something I could share with others, and I started to coach other guys on how to do the same for themselves. My coaching business grew quickly, and over the course of a few years, I worked with more than ten thousand guys on how to attract women. By trying to overcome my own limitations I wound up developing a widespread reputation throughout the United Kingdom for helping guys with their love lives. I was featured in a major documentary and dubbed in the press as a real-life Hitch, after the 2005 romantic comedy starring Will Smith as a professional "date doctor."

One day I was giving a talk to a room full of three hundred guys, and to break the ice I asked, "So, who here wants to get laid?" There wasn't a single woman in the room. There was no reason for them to be anything but honest. You would think they would all raise their hands. What guy *doesn't* want to get laid, right? But only 60 percent of them raised their hands. Then I asked, "Who here wants to find a great relationship?" And do you know what happened? Every single hand in the room went up.

It turns out that men want what women want: a lasting, meaningful relationship.

I couldn't stop thinking about that show of hands. If women knew this about men, I thought, it might make them feel more optimistic about finding true love.

At first, the thought of coaching women seemed daunting. How could I possibly understand a woman's point of view? Why would anyone listen to me? I'm a guy. How could I possibly help? But then the idea struck me that I *knew* what guys were thinking. I had spent years learning about what makes guys tick and what they were looking for. What if I took all of that acquired intelligence and shared it with women so they could use it to find love? I could help them get noticed, get dates, and get treated with respect. Perhaps I could even help them to get the proposal of marriage so many of my female friends thought was out of reach.

I created some basic and practical steps for women to follow and then hosted a small gathering for the women in my life. At this meeting, I distilled and divulged what I'd learned about the way men think and how women could use this to their advantage. We worked on elegant techniques the women could use to influence men without ever looking as if they were doing anything. I offered subtle ways in which they could be proactive in their love lives, ways that would slip completely under a guy's radar, so that they could choose the guy they wanted and orchestrate his attraction.

The key to making it all work is striking the perfect balance between being proactive and being high value. (There's plenty in this book on the subject of being a high-value woman. More about that later.)

I had no idea how this would all go over, but my friends were floored. They'd never heard these things before, certainly never from a guy. In some ways, I felt as if I was betraying my own sex by coming over to fight for the other side, but I really wanted to bring some assistance to my female friends. Even though I believed every word of what I told these women, what happened next was crazy.

Within the next week my single friends began getting dates with men who appealed to them. Those in relationships started saying their boyfriends were treating them with more respect, admiration, and attraction. Men who had never said, "I love you" started saying it for the first time; one even proposed, though previously he had said he never would. Three months later, the women who'd been single were in relationships with guys they adored.

Word spread. Women I didn't know started calling me, asking for advice. E-mails flooded my inbox from women with dating and relationship questions. I began conducting private coaching sessions. Every week, I'd receive phone calls at all hours of the night from women in far-flung time zones.

This was the beginning of what would be a years-long journey of working with fifty thousand women in Get the Guy events, and with millions online, to help them find love. Through Get the Guy, I now host everything from weekend events aimed at transforming women's love lives to transformative five-day retreats held all over the world. The contents of this book are the result of what I have been thinking about, teaching, and refining over the past four years.

During the Get the Guy weekend course, I give women the A to Z on everything they need to know, from where to meet the right guys and how to attract them, to how to make the guy they've chosen desire a relationship that will last a lifetime. I've utilized thousands of real-life case studies to road test every technique and theory. My mission is to share every piece of secret information about men that I have been privy to in order to transform women's love lives.

The evening of the first day of the event, I send these women out into the world with a simple mission to practice everything they'd learned that day. They talk, flirt, and have fun in ways they'd never experienced. The next morning they return to the seminar and recount their stories. Women who haven't had a date in years tell of how they already have several dates set up for the next week. It is my hope that you will do the same after reading this book.

Get the Guy is meant to be a double entendre. It will help you land a mate, if that's what you desire, but it will also help you "get" the guy—to understand how men think, what they really want, how they view women, relationships, sex, and commitment. However, even though I reveal a lot of secrets about the male mind, this book isn't about guys, it's about you. There's nothing I say here that isn't designed to help you. Some of it might strike you as a little blunt, but were I writing a book for men I would be just as direct about what they should be doing to find women, and believe me, the book would be much longer. While I can't help you by telling you what's wrong with men, I can help by telling you how to utilize men's needs and desires to find the one worthy of your love. Think of me as your personal insider, the guy in your corner.

I know there is a lot of information out there about how to improve your love life. There's the makeover crowd, who focus on fixing your appearance to the exclusion of your behavior, and the therapy crowd, who delve into your deepest psychological and emotional barriers to help you overcome obstacles. These are the shallow and deep ends of the spectrum and may well have value. But what you really need to know are the logistics necessary to go about finding, meeting, and getting the guy, and then what to do with him once you've got him.

With a proper model, you will be successful. No matter who you are, what you look like, what you do for work, whether you've been married before, whether you have kids, whether you're shy or outgoing, tall or short, blond or redhead, you can have the kind of love life you desire. It has nothing to do with luck or fate or Cupid showing up with bow and arrow. Your love life is not determined by romantic notions and magical thinking, but rather by a set of conditions that everyone and anyone can create.

My model is based on three basic ideas:

1. Learning simple, new behaviors that allow you to meet more guys and choose those you like

2. Understanding how men think and what they want

3. Creating a high-value lifestyle that will draw men to you and satisfy you with or without your guy

The book is organized by techniques for finding the guy, getting the guy, and keeping the guy.

"Finding the Guy" will teach you how to meet more men, get them to approach you, and engage in conversation that will tell you within minutes whether you want to get to know a guy better. This part of the book focuses primarily on how to increase your odds of meeting the right guy. While some of it may seem daunting, it's the millimeter shifts in behavior that transform our lives and love lives.

"Getting the Guy" deals with methods for creating attraction and deepening your connection to find out if this is a guy you want in your life.

Finally, "Keeping the Guy" focuses on the work that we all have to do when we finally find the love of our life. You will learn that the theories that apply in the beginning are also relevant at the end. The practices you develop and hold dear will help you to enjoy the love life you've been hoping for.

One last note: As you go through the book you'll see sidebars that contain links to online videos designed to help you visualize the techniques in the book. If you don't have online access, or you are not inclined to move off the page, the book stands on its own.

However, I wanted to overdeliver for you, so I have taken strategic snippets from my live seminars—which women fly from all over the world to attend—and put them online. In these videos, I speak directly to you with the hope that your reading experience is enhanced, and you get the most from this book.

If you'd like to get started with these videos immediately, **go to www.gettheguybook.com/members and enter the code: gtgbook.** And here is my promise to you: if you read this book, watch the videos, and truly put the advice into practice, you will meet more guys, your love life will improve, and ultimately so will your life. So let's get started!

PART ONE

Find the Guy

1

===

Put the Odds in Your Favor

How many guys do you meet in an average week?

And when I say "meet," I refer to a genuine social interaction, where you engage with a man, eye contact and all, for anywhere from five minutes of chatting to a full two-hour conversation. But it has to *be* a conversation, not just collecting your mail from the postman (unless of course *he's* new and you turn him into a social connection).

If your answer is none, or even one, how long do you think it's going to take you to meet *the* guy? I'm going to give you the benefit of the doubt: let's say you meet one new man every week. How long will it take to meet Mr. Right if you are meeting only one new man in an average week? I'm not a mathematician, but the odds are pretty long. What makes them even longer is that these interactions are probably happening by chance, and certainly not because they are men you have selected yourself.

This isn't the case for only you. If I asked the same question of a male reader, the number would be just as small. Both sexes are guilty of leaving their love lives to chance. Blame it on the fairy tales we're read as kids, blame it on Hollywood, but the fact remains that we've come to believe that true love is the product of fate. We've all been led to believe that someday it will just "happen," that one day fate will drop the person of our dreams right next to us while we're standing at a stoplight. The fate-will-bring-me-love approach lacks urgency, which leads to lack of action. You assume that "when the time is right" the right guy will come along, and in the meantime you focus on your work, your ambitions, your family, your friends, your hobbies. That's not to say that these are not all highly fulfilling aspects of your life in their own right, but I want to help you understand how within these essential parts of your life are opportunities to find the man of your dreams. When people put aside their love life to focus on these other areas, years pass, and one day the lack of urgency turns into panic. We become frantic as we realize that not only is nothing happening in our love life, but we are at a loss as to *how* to make it happen, which of course leads to more panic, creating a loop of frustration, at best, or worse, hopelessness. You may be reading this book because you keep asking yourself (and perhaps your sisters, girlfriends, and coworkers), "Where are all the good men to be found?" If you're gradually coming to the realization that fate isn't cooperating, you might be on the verge of seeing that you're going to have to be proactive. You are going to have to go out and find him.

And how do you find him?

It's a very simple principle:

To meet more men you have to, er, meet more men!

Waiting or Creating

A word of encouragement before you set out to meet the man of your dreams: Life is full of people who wait. They wait for the right moment to approach someone, or wait for someone to approach them first. They wait for someone to show enough interest that they don't risk being rejected, they wait to be invited, and they wait to make a move. They wait to feel confident before taking action. Wait, wait, wait, for everything.

"Waiters" imagine they are playing it safe, but more often than not, only two things come to those who wait: the wrong thing or no-thing.

Ask yourself: Right now, at this very moment, am I waiting or am I creating? Am I taking the positive steps which will give me results in my love life? (If your answer is no, take heart; simply by reading this book you are already taking action, seeking the knowledge that will enable you to make the changes necessary to make rapid progress.)

There's an added benefit to taking your life into your own hands: when you know you are doing everything in your power to improve your situation, you can be content even if the results aren't immediate. The knowledge that you are moving forward, improving, and developing in a significant way is what makes humans happy.

Wherever you feel you are right now, you still have a choice: you can wait or you can create.

There is only one way to wait: just do nothing. But there are thousands of ways to create, so the opportunities are endless.

START CREATING NOW

I've produced a special video to help you start creating.

Go to **www.gettheguybook.com/create**
Access code: **gtgbook**

Throwing the Net Wide

I know your goal is not to meet as many men as possible, but to meet *your* man, the one who is going to add more meaning to your life. Setting aside for a moment the logic that you can't meet your man if you don't meet any men, there is another reason to throw the net wide.

Let's say that you meet only one man in three years. You might think he is fine—or, even better, perfect for you. But since you have nothing to compare him with, you risk settling for less than you deserve. No one is perceptive enough to call it correctly with only one choice.

As much as you might love to act like a marksman, picking out a single target, taking aim, and shooting, you can't just pick your ideal man out of the crowd with Cupid's single shot. I suspect you've already discovered on occasion that even when you think you have hit the bull's-eye, you have instead missed the mark completely! A single shot does not allow you to choose the best for yourself. And, you never, ever want to settle.

If you want to have a better chance of finding the right guy, you have to begin with meeting more men. Not one more, not two more, but a *lot* more. The more men you meet, the more you increase your chances of finding the right one.

Imagine attending a party where there are two hundred men in the room. Out of these two hundred guys, how many would you feel even remotely attracted to? Maybe twenty? Out of this twenty, there might be only ten to whom you felt enough attraction to consider a first date. From this remaining ten, how many would you feel sufficient chemistry with to want to date again? Five? And from these five last men standing, there may be only one with whom you could deeply connect. Many might say that even these figures are wildly optimistic. In which case, how long will it take to find your guy if you're meeting only one new man each week? Anywhere from four years to . . . you won't live that long. In this scenario, you're left relying on fate, which is like hoping to get rich playing the lottery.

Time Out: Reality Check

I'm not a mind reader, but I do have quite a bit of experience hearing directly from women some common complaints about men that simply are not true. I want to share a collection of stubborn myths about guys and love that refuse to go away. These mad and bad beliefs do you no good and only hold you back:

- ✦ There are no good men out there ("All the men I meet are either gay, taken, or weird").

- ✦ Guys only want someone hotter and prettier than me.

- ✦ Guys don't like women who approach them first.

- ✦ Guys only want a low-maintenance woman, not someone who will challenge them.

- ✦ Guys don't want to commit, they only want casual flings and sex.

Every single one of these is a myth. Sadly, they are not only false, but they are dangerous to hold on to and often become excuses for all that is wrong in your love life.

Most of us have had painful experiences in love. It's one of life's biggest, most unforgettable experiences. Love hurts, as the song says. But when we have been let down by someone, we have to be careful not to let that experience, however awful, become our sole reference point for future relationships.

I'll make you a deal. If you set aside all the myths and generalizations, if you set aside whatever bad experiences you may have had with men and refuse to allow them to color your judgment, I will reveal to you all the facets and secrets of the male mind, the good, the bad, and all the things he desires from the woman in his life.

The Philosophy of the Funnel

Now that you are committed to expanding your options by meeting a lot more men, I am going to offer a proven system, a method to all of this man-meeting. It is a process best visualized as a series of funnels.

The first funnel is the largest, into which you pour all the new men you meet. (We'll get to the part about how you are going to meet all these new men in a few pages . . . stay with me.) The funnel acts as a filter, and only the guys you're attracted to pass through to the second funnel.

The second funnel then filters out all the guys you don't want to date. These would be the guys who may seem attractive at first glance, but you don't have any immediate chemistry with them for you to want to make real time for them. Only those guys you're genuinely interested in spending time with drop into the third funnel. Of those, only a select few will pass into the fourth funnel, those who are worth more than just one date. Of course the final filtering will result in finding the guy with whom you want a relationship. We will dig into that process in the second and third parts of the book. For now, we are simply getting you to the place of opportunity.

The process is clear and obvious, but there is one important principle I want to emphasize: the first funnel is where we are *least* selective. The first funnel is not about attraction. It is about meeting new people, both men and women.

The first funnel is about getting out there. It's about joining the human race. It's about practicing conversation and flirting. It's about interacting and entertaining and allowing ourselves to be entertained. Out into the world you go, with the goal of meeting as many guys as possible, so that you have more guys to pour into the first funnel. Pouring only three guys into that first funnel makes it highly unlikely that the right guy will come out the other end. Pouring in every guy who doesn't strike you as a potential serial killer makes your chances much higher that at the end the right one will emerge.

Part of the reason you're tossing every guy into the first funnel is to create the habit of giving a lot of guys a chance, early on. Most of us are so focused on meeting The One that we wind up not meeting anyone. If I could, I would tattoo this on your palm: every interaction with another human being is a possible gateway to some new world or experience, which could, in turn, introduce you to the love of your life.

There are other good reasons to meet as many men as you can:

Abundance, not scarcity

When you meet lots of men, you put less focus on any one man. Approaching your love life from a position of abundance rather than scarcity helps to put the odds in your favor. It is making simple economics work for you.

As much as you might be agonizing over one guy, always remember, men are 50 percent of the population. You are not the luckiest woman in the world when you meet one you like, and you aren't the unluckiest woman in the world when the guy you like doesn't like you back. Scarcity makes us settle. If you believe that there aren't many good guys out there, you'll invest far too much in the first decent man you *do* meet, even if he's far from being the right one. Abundance, on the other hand, leads to choice and confidence. Abundance comes when we start increasing the number of men going into that first funnel. As soon as you heartily believe that there are plenty of men out there, you can adopt an easy come, easy go attitude and begin to have fun with all of this.

Creating new habits

Make a habit of talking to new people. It will do wonders for increasing your basic social skills, which will in turn boost your confidence. You will find yourself creating attraction simply by becoming more at ease engaging with someone you don't know or whom you've just met. This happens simply by doing it more often, and applies not only for men but for anyone at all: women, children, young and old. If you are in the habit of meeting more people in general, it will by default lead you to meet more men. Why do you think you revert back to a being a blushing, nervous schoolgirl when that hot guy approaches you? Because you're out of practice. You can't instantly summon your best, most confident self for the hot guy if you've never developed your skills by talking to everyone.

Because you're choosing

The more new men you meet, the more you'll have to choose from. This will allow you to be selective. We should all be extremely fussy when it comes to love. The person you spend most of your time with, are intimate with, share your life with, and whom you trust the most needs to be extraordinary for you specifically. There are extraordinary people everywhere, but it will take some filtering to find that certain someone who fills your particular needs and desires. Logically, then, to find that special person, you will need to increase your chances of success by meeting many men.

═══

The idea of treating our love life like a large filter system might not seem like the most romantic approach to the dating process, but as we've seen, leaving it to fate also leaves us with no sense of agency in our lives. The fact that we can apply workable strategies to create the results we want doesn't make our love, once we find it, any less real, meaningful, sexy, or romantic.

Yes, I know. Some people do get lucky.

I once knew a young woman named Jane who, while sitting in her first college class waiting for the lecturer to arrive, met the love of her life. An attractive and friendly young man happened to sit down right next to her. They joked together, and went for coffee after the lecture. A month later they were seeing each other regularly and ultimately began a relationship that lasted throughout her university years. She told all her friends that he was The One. She envisaged getting married at twenty-five, with kids to follow a couple of years later. She had it all planned out. Her friends were a little envious. They wondered how it was so easy for her.

Then one day, Jane's boyfriend, The One, tells told her he needed to do his own thing for a while. He wasn't ready for marriage, and though he loved her, there was so much more he felt he needed to do before settling down. All of a sudden, at age twenty-five, Jane found herself back in the dating game, heartbroken and wondering where and how she would ever meet someone again.

She patiently waited for another Mr. Right to come along, but nothing happened. She daydreamed that perhaps the guy sitting at the next desk at her new job would be attractive and friendly and introduce himself, just as her first love did. Then, when she began the job, not only was the guy in the next desk neither friendly nor attractive, he didn't even bother to make conversation. She spent Friday and Saturday nights going out with her friends, talking about how impossible it was to find someone like the man she once had. She had won the lottery of love at eighteen and spent seven years enjoying the winnings. But at twenty-five she was bankrupt, and now she was seven years older without any idea how to get back out there. Because her limited experience had taught her that the right man was supposed to sit down next to you and start a relationship with you on an unexpected day, she had no skills to make it happen.

Most lottery winners (even those who win millions) find a way to go broke again. And when they do go broke, they don't know how to make that money again because when it happened the first time it was by pure chance. They have no formula they can replicate. Those who are successful in business, on the other hand, know that going broke isn't the end of the world. They have the skills to get back into the game and create something from nothing, and know that waiting will get them nowhere. Likewise, those who know how to go out and find a relationship don't panic when they're single.

Jane thought her only option was to sit around and wait.

Nonsense.

Rituals: The Best-Kept Secret of the Successful

Rituals are the best-kept secret of anyone who has ever succeeded in business, love, fitness, family life, learning a foreign language, or any other area. The dictionary says a ritual is an "action or type of behavior regularly and invariably followed," or alternatively, an "action that is repeated continuously in the same way." Rituals are usually enacted for positive results. Following rituals creates a positive association, which in turn results in a positive outcome. I often quote Keith Cunningham's simple but effective mantra: "Ordinary things done consistently produce extraordinary results." This is as true in our love life as in every other aspect of our lives.

The rituals that we are looking at here are designed specifically to help you meet more men.

Increasing the number of new men you meet each week—from,

say, one to three or four—would have a dramatic impact on your love life in just a few months. Four new men each week equals two hundred new men in a year. That incremental weekly increase would totally transform the entire landscape of your dating.

How would your life have to change right now if you set yourself the challenge of meeting two hundred new guys in the next twelve months? Not *date* two hundred guys, just *meet* two hundred. Some of them might lead to dates, but for now, imagine just starting a five-minute conversation with two hundred new guys this year. What would you have to do differently? How would you have to spend your time differently from the way you spend it now?

Sustainable change is rarely created by one huge action with dramatic results. In fact, it's just the opposite. What is essential is that the process is natural and easy to assimilate, so that our love life takes care of itself while still letting us go about our normal routine. Since it is so easy to make small changes for a big return, you can take control of your love life beginning today.

I get frustrated by TV shows that take a woman with no confidence and no social life, who has difficulty finding a relationship, and claim they are going to give her an instant total makeover and turn her into a new woman. They then busy themselves changing her makeup, hairstyle, and wardrobe —all of which results only in a change in appearance.

The implication is that all that was missing from her life was that her look needed updating. I have nothing against working on how we look; establishing rituals that maintain our health, fitness, and physical appearance has great value, but on their own these will produce no more than a small shift in our love life. It may be a positive step forward, but it's still a baby step.

The effects of such a makeover are temporary. It works on our external appearance and might look like a big transformation on screen, but it doesn't target the changes in behavior that really make the difference. Yes, I know it can be great TV, but no speedy external makeover addresses the greater task at hand of finding (and keeping) the right man for you.

So, what are those rituals that will put you on the right path to your man? And how do we enact them? Read on.

Meet New People Everywhere

The key is to learn how to create conversations everywhere we go. Here are some rituals we can implement to ensure that we constantly exercise these social muscles.

Converse with all service staff

Make a habit of talking to everyone who serves you: wait staff, baristas, salespeople, doormen, the UPS man. This is great practice, especially if you're shy, because talking to *you* is part of their job. Try to make every conversation go one step further. Aim to get their names, or find out where they live, or find out one simple fact about them.

You can always ask anyone in any situation, "How's your day going?" When he replies, follow up with another question, a comment about the weather, or even a compliment. Tell him something nice about his smile for no reason other than to make him feel good. If he has an accent, ask where he's from. If it's Friday, ask him if he's doing anything fun this weekend. Ask him to recommend his favorite kind of cake, or if you're ordering coffee, ask him if he can make one of those artistic designs on the foam.

Service staff are supposed to be nice to you, so take advantage of it. It's great practice and it will make their day—and yours—so much better.

Learn the names of the regular people in your life

Whether it's the guy who hands out the towels at the gym, the person who serves you lunch, or the security guard at your office, make a mission to get a new name from someone every day.

Talk to anyone reading a book

Speak to anyone you see holding a book you have read or want to read. Comment on it or ask if they've read any of the author's other books. You could simply ask if they are enjoying it or whether they would recommend it.

Talk to any guy playing with an iPad (or any other gadget)

Chatting with a guy about his gadgets is easy. Every guy loves to show them off and tell you all about them. Ask him what his favorite app is, or what model he recommends getting, or what the best thing about it is.

In the coffee shop, talk to the person next to you in line

You could ask him to move away so you can grab something off a shelf, or you could ask if he would hold your umbrella while you fish out your wallet from your purse. If you're feeling really adventurous, ask him his position on skim versus whole milk for coffee.

You can't leave the gym until you've had three conversations

Speak with another customer, with a staff member, and with a personal trainer (or have three conversations all in one go with the people you meet at a kickboxing class).

Compliment three people a day

Clothing, shoes, and eyeglasses are easy to compliment (within reason, of course . . . you wouldn't want to compliment a muddy pair of boots, lest he think you're being snarky!). Eyeglasses are great to compliment, because it gives you a reason to look directly into someone's eyes. Hats too, since they force you to look up, not down at someone's shoes.

Provide a random act of kindness to one person each day

Hold the door open for someone. If you are driving, smile and let another car go ahead of you in traffic. Help an elderly person cross the street. Buy someone you barely know a cup of coffee. Even exchanges seemingly unrelated to our love life have a cumulative effect on our confidence and our ease with spontaneous interactions.

If you struggle to talk to any strangers, start small. Ask a guy for the time, or just hold eye contact and say, "Hey, how are you today?" If this is easy, go straight to asking an opinion about something that's on your mind. Or assign yourself a challenge, like offering a compliment or asking for a phone number whenever you're in a conversation with a new guy for more than five minutes.

All these rituals can be built into your everyday life. They might seem small, but it is foolish to underestimate the power of small actions undertaken with regularity. The state of your love life one year from now will be a direct reflection of the rituals you set for yourself today.

Over the course of our lives most of us meet a fraction of the people we could have met. You can probably already think of someone wonderful who has been in your life only because at one point you took a chance and made conversation with him or her. These actions are small in the moment, but they can have enormous consequences.

Remember to create rituals that require you to perform a specific action. An abstract commandment like "be more sociable" is unlikely to translate into action because you have no criteria for judging whether you are maintaining the ritual. Within one week of adopting these specific new behavioral rituals, you will feel (and look) like a social animal, even though it requires so little effort within your daily routine.

The Perfect Time to Start Is Now

The French philosopher Voltaire said one of the wisest things I've ever heard: "Don't let the perfect be the enemy of the good." In other words, nothing is gained by waiting until all the circumstances are just right before we take any action, because the circumstances are never *just* right. Taking action now is what is required; we get more results from action than we do from waiting.

We decide that we can't talk to that person yet because he's with friends, or he hasn't smiled at us yet. This kind of procrastination is common. It is easy to justify inactivity this way. We decide to get our body in shape, but instead of taking action now, we wait because we don't have all the gym gear, we are too busy this week, we will start when we feel less tired, when we can dedicate more time to it . . . and before we know it, because we've been waiting for the perfect time, another year passes and still we have made no progress.

This goes for meeting men as well.

Suppose you set yourself a new ritual of talking to two new men on the way to work every day for the next year. Let's say optimistically, that on the fiftieth day of doing this you meet a man who turns out to be the love of your life. Later, when you look back on that story of how you met one fateful day on the way to work, your friends will say, "Gosh, you got so lucky. You met him randomly on the way to work one day." Yet you will know you weren't just lucky, or rather, that you put yourself in the path of luck. You were only lucky in the sense that he happened to be there on a particular day. But luck isn't what got you the result. What enabled you to meet him was the new ritual you had established. You found love because you set out to find love and made it happen.

ADOPTING THE RIGHT MINDSET

By now you're probably a little amped up but wondering if you're going to have the motivation to really put these ideas to the test in your everyday life. This next video is intended to help instill in you the right mindset before you get too far in.

Go to **www.gettheguybook.com/mindset**
Access code: **gtgbook**

2

===

Being a Woman of High Value

In order to attract extraordinary people, we have to be extraordinary. And we have to be extraordinary not only for others, we have to do it for ourselves.

Getting the guy starts with raising your game, raising your standards, and understanding from the start that you are a woman of high value.

What do I mean by a woman of high value?

Aristotle said, "We are what we repeatedly do." If we want to embody and exhibit our best qualities, we have to be living them. I recently asked my friend Sylvia what kind of man she was looking for and she reeled off a list of terrific qualities. The man of her dreams would be outgoing, with great friends. He would be honest, bold, adventurous, with direction and purpose, passion and confidence. He would know what he wanted out of life and live up to his own high standards. In other words, Sylvia wants someone extraordinary.

Sylvia's my friend, so of course I think she's pretty great, but the point is this: How many traits that you long for in your perfect man do you embody yourself? Because believe me, Mr. Right, wherever he is out there, wants the same thing. In the same way you're not sitting sipping your tea and thinking, What I'd really like is a dullard who has no inner life and will look to me to fulfill all his needs and make his life exciting, Mr. Right is hoping to find a woman of high value.

That's you.

Obviously, we all possess our own unique personalities, our own individual likes and dislikes, our own opinions, specific things that drive us mad or make us laugh, but there are traits that all high-value women possess. They are self-confidence, independence, integrity, and femininity. Cultivating these traits is the first step toward finding the love you deserve.

Self-Confidence

Certainty is the primary attribute of the high-value woman.

The definition of confidence is the state of feeling certain about the truth of something, and the high-value woman is confident about her worth. She knows her abilities, her appeal, and what she deserves. A woman who is certain about herself has a deep feeling of self-worth that informs all her other attributes. If she is not getting what she wants or needs from a relationship, the self-confident woman will feel comfortable articulating her needs or walking away from a less-than-fulfilling union. This is true in the earliest stages of meeting guys as well—if the man you are talking to is boring the hell out of you, or a blowhard, a self-confident woman will politely extricate herself instead of wasting her time.

Displaying self-confidence can be playful. Not long ago I was in Los Angeles, heading to the airport to catch a flight. Minutes after I was collected by a cab, the driver caught my eye in his rearview mirror and said, "Someone must think very highly of you."

"Why's that?" I said.

"Because they sent you *me*!" he said, without missing a beat.

I remember thinking, This is so cool. This guy is so secure in himself. He wasn't looking for my approval, he just declared his worth in a cheeky way with a smile, as though it were a matter of fact. This, I thought, is exactly the kind of confidence people should have. Not arrogant, not full of self-importance, but relaxed and a little amused about how sensational we know ourselves to be.

Certainty turns out to be one of the sexiest qualities you can possess. A woman with certainty knows that any man's life would be immeasurably improved for having her in it. She knows for a fact that when the right guy does come along, committing to her will be the best decision he will ever make in his life.

I once watched a documentary about a couple who had been happily married for forty years. It was obvious that even after all these years they were still in love. She looked at him with a twinkle in her eye and said, "I saved you, you know. You were so lucky! No one could have pleased you as I did. If another woman had gotten you she wouldn't have known what to do with you." At that moment I knew exactly why he was crazy about her, even after forty years. She knew with absolute certainty that she was the best thing that ever happened to him.

The self-confident woman is comfortable in social situations, even if she is shy. When this woman goes to a party, she's secure in her own desirability. She doesn't waste her time comparing herself with other women, or trying to blend in, or looking to others to dictate how she's going to behave. If another woman attracts attention because of her looks, it doesn't make her feel badly about herself. There is always going to be someone richer, thinner, smarter, and better looking— and thank goodness, that doesn't matter. She's unaffected by superficial things. She is neither intimidated nor overly impressed because a guy has looks, money, or high status. She knows that she is worth more than all of these things.

Uncertain people are followers, looking to others for approval. Frightened to say what they feel in case others don't feel the same, they adapt to fit in with everyone else. You may have once believed that being compliant is appealing to men because it is a quality that won't intimidate them. But the truth is that nothing snuffs out attraction quicker than when a guy picks up on uncertainty. When he senses that you are doing something out of character just to try to please him, he will sense it is because you feel unworthy of him. Being "nice" will not compel him to choose you over other women in the room. Confidence trumps compliance every time. Here's why: if you are certain of your self-worth and you are speaking with him, then he feels special. So your self-confidence becomes a mirror for his sense of self. This is true of most interactions with other people, but it is especially true of romantic interactions between men and women.

Women are better at reading body signals, better at sensing the mood of the room, better at interpreting pretty much all nonverbal cues, but a guy can always sense when a women is uncertain of herself. He can feel insecurity a mile away. Generally speaking, a confident and secure man will lose interest in a woman if he senses insecurity. Don't give him reasons not to be interested. Save your self-doubt for a therapist.

A woman who is certain knows what she is looking for in a man and never settles for less than her highest standards. She thinks, If a guy can't meet my needs, he's not right for me. When a guy is around this kind of woman, he wants to bring his A-game, knowing she won't accept less. He wants the woman who already knows that she is good enough for him.

Independence

===

Before you get the guy you've got to get a life.

Independence and self-determination are important traits of the high-value woman. She has a life that she adores and is engaged in meaningful activities that make her passionate about each day. She may have a job she loves, but she also fills her leisure time with activities that appeal to her creatively and emotionally. She surrounds herself with people who reinforce her values and her confidence. She doesn't rely on a man to be entertained. Her life is her own.

This advice applies to your life with or without a man. It all connects back to the issue of being choosy. If your life is brimming, you won't be looking for a man to fill a void. In that way you can be more selective about the man you decide gets to spend time with you. A fuller life will help you choose your man wisely.

So what is a guy thinking when he meets an independent woman? He wants in. He wants to be part of her fabulous life—but at the same time he isn't afraid that she will become too needy. One of the most common male fears about relationships is the fear of being smothered. A man worries that once he's in a relationship he's going to lose his own life. You can approach this male instinct by appealing to his ego: you welcome him to be part of your life. At the same time, you don't push to be part of every single thing he does. If there is part of how you fill your day that he'd rather abstain from—maybe he doesn't want to do yoga, rock climb, go shopping, or hang with your platonic male friends—then you can happily continue those activities without him. Your message to him: I am a complete person without you, but I desire to have you be a part of my life because you are worthy of it.

The tricky thing to balance here is to maintain your independence but also help him feel that he brings something to the table—and if you have found the right guy, that shouldn't be too difficult. (If you can't answer the question about what he brings to your wonderful life in less than a minute—get out!) While you don't have to spend all your time stroking his ego, acknowledgment and appreciation of his interests go a long way.

Integrity

A woman with integrity sticks to her principles.

Having integrity is about knowing what your own standards are and being completely comfortable with them. A woman of integrity doesn't compromise what she believes in simply in order to seek approval from others, nor does she let bad behavior slide in order to try to fit in. If she finds someone she is attracted to, she won't recalibrate her values to match his. This is true for large issues and for small ones. It's about being loyal to your friends, not being overly critical of others, and refraining from harmful gossip. It is also being polite to staff at a restaurant and considerate about where you use your cell phone. These actions, large and small, set you apart as a woman of high value. Like confidence, integrity is not only an attractive trait to men, but one that ought to be cultivated for your best self.

For purposes of getting the guy, integrity sends a message to a man that he can expect you to hold steady to your values, which establishes trust. When a man trusts you, he will listen more attentively and know that what you say has real weight. If your interactions come from a place of integrity, then you set up a dynamic where you can expect the same from your man. Face it, a woman of real integrity is not going to put up with a guy who lacks it. Holding fast to your own integrity helps him to know what you expect of him, and he feels challenged to not disappoint you.

Femininity

Don't stop being a girl.

There, I said it. I realize I may be entering a minefield, but I might as well get it out of the way. I'm not talking about gender equality here, or your right to work as a firefighter for the exact same pay as a man, or the need for men to help balance the division of labor by pitching in and doing more vacuuming and diaper changing.

Femininity and issues of equality have become so confused that it feels hazardous to even have the conversation. But I want to clear up some common misconceptions. I often hear women comment on how being strong and independent is intimidating to a guy. This might be true sometimes, but as we've just discussed, any man worthy of your attention and affection is looking for those very qualities. However, that doesn't mean that you need to lose your femininity at the same time. In fact, I will say that your biggest strength may well be your preternatural ability to be a woman! We are living in a time when women make up a larger percentage of the workforce than ever before. You are financially independent, because many of the cultural and social barriers preventing women from gaining parity have broken down. Women no longer need men to provide and protect. Through all of these incredibly positive advancements, men and women seem to be confused about how this shift in roles affects notions of masculinity and femininity. However, one thing remains as true as it ever was: the thing that a man finds attractive, on a fundamental level, is a woman's femininity. Regardless of who's bringing home the bacon or dropping the kids off at day care, men are hardwired to respond to the feminine in women. And if we're being completely honest, the reason this is so is because we men need women to help us feel masculine. You can call it yin and yang, or two pieces of a puzzle. Whatever metaphor, there is something essential about the attraction between the sexes.

Every man needs to feel as if he provides something a woman couldn't live without. He doesn't need to feel this in a literal sense. He doesn't need to go to bed at night thinking, Ah, but for me, Sarah would have no one to change the oil in her car. But he does need to feel it emotionally. It satisfies his instinct to provide and protect.

This doesn't mean he has to be the breadwinner. Just because a man is born with an instinct to provide, it doesn't mean that he has to provide financially. The truth is, what emasculates men is when they feel like they don't provide anything. Once broken, the male ego is difficult to fix.

The woman of high value is confident and independent, but she also is wise enough to know (and happy to admit) that there are certain things only a guy, her guy, can provide. Sure, she might sit in a bar with her girlfriends and join in the familiar refrain, "Men! Who needs them?" but the truth is, she doesn't believe it.

When guys hear that you don't need men, that you can do "everything" yourself, it doesn't make him think you're sassy and self-sufficient. It doesn't make him marvel at how bad-ass you are. It just makes him feel useless.

And make no mistake, no guy can handle the idea of being with someone for whom he is useless.

So the issue of femininity does not work in contrast to confidence and independence, but rather as the starting point for these traits. A woman who knows who she is, strong and independent, understands how essential it is to show that she needs her guy in other ways. If you come home from work, hug him as tight as you can, give him a super sexy kiss and say, "I really missed you today" or "I couldn't wait to see you all day," suddenly he gets that buzz that appeals to the provider in him. Because now he matters. Even though he sees you as being strong and capable, you still need him. And who doesn't need to be needed?

I rarely deal in absolutes. We're all individuals, and relationships are mutable and fluid. But I do have one hard and fast rule. If you're ever out on a date, whether it be the first or the hundredth, and you're strolling along, the breeze picks up, it seems as if the temperature is dropping, and the guy offers his jacket, just take it.

You might not be cold. You might be enjoying the breeze on your arms. You might think the guy's jacket is unspeakably hideous. Just take it.

Don't say, "I'm fine, thanks."

Don't say, "I'm a little cold, but you must be too."

Don't say, "No, really, I'm fine."

Just. Take. The. Friggin'. Jacket. Whether you are cold or not.

Let him come to your rescue. When he offers you his jacket, this isn't his attempt to be patronizing. This is your guy wanting to feel like he's able to serve you. This is what makes him feel like a man. Men live to serve women on a level that most men will never admit to and most women will never understand.

When a man offers to carry your suitcase, it's not because he thinks that without his bulging manly arms holding your luggage you'll be a helpless damsel in distress just waiting for someone to heave your bags up those stairs.

In that moment, when you're standing at the bottom of your apartment steps with your suitcase, he is not implying that you are insignificant or weak. He is simply trying to make himself feel accepted. A woman accepting his help is a woman accepting *him*. It's you saying, "Okay, you're *allowed* to take care of me." He knows you don't need to be taken care of, but on some level he wants to be able to take care of your needs. A woman of high value knows this and permits it. *It's not about you and your power, it's about him and his insecurity.*

———

All of the qualities we discuss in this chapter have to do with character. A high-value woman is a woman with strong character. She may be shy, but she still has confidence. Her life may be quiet and simple or glamorous and raucous, but she is fulfilled and independent. She may

like to chop wood or race motorbikes, but she never loses her femininity. And she always, always sticks to her principles, even in the face of
adversity. Adopting and developing the traits of a high-value woman
will contribute to the basic quality of your life, and it will move you
to a place where you love every day, whether you're in a relationship
or not.

The best life is one in which we're excited to wake up in the morning. When we have that, we "win" no matter what happens in our
love life. With or without a person to share it with, we have a passionate, fun, exciting, emotionally fulfilling, and extraordinary existence.
Whatever happens, we become extraordinary, and the truth becomes
clear: we don't enter relationships hoping to create an extraordinary
existence; we come to them to share one with someone else.

Being a high-value woman will ensure that you find just such a
relationship.

Dating will become easier because you'll always have something
fun to do. Because you already have interests and passions, you won't
have to scratch your head to come up with an interesting activity when
a guy suggests "doing something."

Also, when someone has a busy, interesting life she adores, she's
unlikely to stake everything on a single guy. She is more confident, because she knows that she is already living a life she's passionate about.

Every relationship starts with a simple conversation, and half of
being an interesting conversationalist is having a life in which you're
fully engaged. When you're enthusiastic about biking or kickboxing
or foreign films or raising goats, you'll never run out of things to talk
about (there's limited mileage in the goat material, but you know what
I mean).

The bottom line is this: women who live passionate lives are inherently sexy. Every guy imagines the girl of his dreams as having
a vibrant, interesting life that he wants to become a part of. He sees
the girl of his dreams as having different sides of her personality he
can explore. She's adventurous, but knows how to relax; outgoing, but

knows how to be cozy and intimate; sexual, but knows how to be sweet. She's got great friends but isn't afraid to go it alone now and then. Maintaining a great lifestyle lets you express and show off and indulge in these different aspects of your character, all of which add up to make you the girl of his dreams.

We have to enjoy every second of the process of building this lifestyle. This should be the most exciting gift we can give ourselves. Imagine your life as a work of art. And with every element you add to it, you are adding another brushstroke to your masterpiece. With every person, every experience, every activity and conversation, you are writing the script for your life. How emotionally exciting and engaging can we make that script? How can we make it a story worth telling?

3

===

Get a Social Life That Serves Your Love Life

Now that we know you are a woman of high value and therefore a real catch for the guy of your dreams, we have to go about the task of finding him. You already know that you have to meet more of them in order to filter out and choose the right guy. Now the issue is where and how. You may be saying, "I barely have time to call my mom on Sundays, so when am I going to have conversations with a bunch of new men?"

I get it. We all have a finite amount of time, and although we will not all enjoy the same number of years in our lives, we all have the same number of hours in a week. Have you spent years promising yourself you'll take that trip or learn that skill or catch up with that old friend when you get the time? And have you? Not having enough time can be our excuse for the rest of our lives if we let it.

Several years ago I took a long, hard look at my own life and realized I had no social life. I didn't come to this realization on my own, mind you: it took an ex-girlfriend to confess that the reason she broke up with me was that I was boring: "All you did was work, or think about work, or plan what you were going to do at work." Boring! Ouch, that hurt.

But she was right. I *had* chosen to spend most of my time and energy developing my business. I could have doubled the hours in a week and still have found work to fill them. Friends would call and without even thinking I would respond, "Busy working tonight, sorry, I can't make it." This response was not just the excuse I gave my friends; I'd started to believe it myself. I had convinced myself that I literally had no hours in the day for a social life.

Some of this was legitimate. I was working extremely hard. But I also knew deep inside that I had attached myself to my work as my go-to excuse for everything else in my life. I made it my get-out-of-jail-free card for avoiding everything challenging, time consuming, or inconvenient. Family commitments, friends, romantic relationships—I had convinced myself that all of these things were just completely impossible. "Lack of time" had become my crutch for every area in which I was not committing. Did I know that I didn't need twenty-four hours a day to work on my business? Yes, obviously, but I still managed to convince myself that I had absolutely no time.

When I'd make an excuse, *even to myself*, I knew it wasn't true. Eventually I realized that I'd clung onto my excuses for so long that I'd started to deny I wanted anything else, including love or a relationship.

Making ourselves busy is often an avoidance activity. We use our busy schedules as a way of excusing and distracting ourselves from addressing issues in our lives that could potentially cause us pain, like seeking a relationship. We unconsciously stuff our schedules with activity just so we can have a reason to excuse the fact that we're still single. It lets us say to our families, our friends, our coworkers, and ourselves: My life is just so busy, I never have time to meet anyone.

None of us truly work twenty-four hours a day, and being busy can't be our excuse forever. We can all think of people in the world who are more successful than we are, busier than we are, with even more demands on their time than ours, who still find time for a relationship. Also, consider this: when our social life—which includes our love life—is nonexistent, the lack of love and connection can poison much of the success we get in other areas of our lives.

My wake-up call came when I took a moment to consider the timeline of my whole life. Visualize the total time you assume you may have on this earth—let's say seventy-five years, barring getting hit by a bus or some other unforeseen calamity—and then subtract all the following elements:

Time in our life already gone

Sleeping hours

Working hours

Time spent on all those chores we can't avoid

Our end years when we may not be fit enough to do things of our choice

It's an eye-opener. What we have left over is a small percentage of our total time in which to do all the things we really want. How are you using this time? Have you realized yet how scarce and therefore precious this time really is?

=====

The idea of changing your lifestyle to give a higher priority to your love life might seem daunting. Perhaps I'm even trying your patience. First, I asked you to give up on the idea that love is a matter of fate deciding when to drop the right guy in front of your nose, and now it feels like I'm asking you to change your entire lifestyle in the interest of finding Mr. Right.

But think of it this way: Why are we happy to spend massive amounts of time working, but flinch at the idea of giving more time to our love life, as though it were unimportant? Do we really think that our love life contributes less to our happiness and fulfillment?

Imagine you were offered the perfect relationship tomorrow. The guy is standing right next to you. He's everything you want in a man: He's attractive, kind, warm, intelligent, and ambitious. He cares about your needs, turns you on sexually, and is fun to be around. He shares all of your deepest values and is dedicated to sharing his life with you. If you were offered this perfect relationship with this perfect person, how much time would you be willing to invest in this relationship each week? How much time would you spend with him? How much time would you spend sharing new experiences with him? How much of your average weekend would you spend being intimate and close to him?

I know the answer: a lot.

Would any of us, if made this offer, reply, "Well, I can only commit one hour a week to this relationship at the most, but no more, because I'm just so busy"? We would *make* time for it, because we know this person is going to make us happy. If we would be willing to invest a lot of time in the perfect relationship, shouldn't we be willing to invest our time in finding such a person?

It's always seemed a bit strange to me that we don't see meeting new people as a priority, yet we prioritize relationships once we are actually in them. We don't think like this about any other area of our lives. No one says that once she gets rich she is going to focus on working hard. Or once she's fit and toned she's going to start going to the gym.

The bottom line is this: if when you find the man of your dreams you are willing to spend so much time with him, doesn't it make sense to be willing to spend the same amount of time doing things that will lead you to him?

The Secret Is in the Social Life

Once you've committed to making time, the question becomes, how can you be more proactive? What do you need to change to bring more people into your life? How do you increase the pool of people from which you'll find that special guy?

It's a mistake to restrict your social circle to just men; everyone you meet has the potential to introduce you to Mr. Right. You may be thinking that your social life is the one area you're quite content with; you already have great friends. You wouldn't be the first one. At my seminars many people approach me at the break and say, "Matt, I don't need help in this area. I have a great life. I have wonderful friends who care about me and enjoy the same activities I do. My problem is I just don't meet any good men!"

But this isn't just about having people you can count on to go out with you for a drink on Saturday night; it's about having a social life that *serves* your love life.

Where the guys are

For a lot of us, our days resemble those of the Bill Murray character in *Groundhog Day*—a mind-numbing routine of eating the same breakfast, going to work, eating the same lunch, at the same time, at the same place, with the same colleagues every day, then going home to watch the same TV programs, before sleeping in preparation for repeating it all again. If your current lifestyle revolves around sitting on the couch on a Saturday night with a glass of wine and watching reality TV shows, then mastering the best techniques for creating attraction with a guy aren't going to matter a lot.

Your challenge, then, isn't just about understanding men, and knowing what to say and how to act or react. To meet more men, you must engage in a lifestyle that brings you into contact with new guys on a regular basis.

The perfect venue for finding men is a myth

Where can I find great men? The question is posed to me so often it's almost as if women believe that there's a secret place, like Narnia or Neverland, where all the good men reside and where their perfect guy is sitting, waiting for them to stumble through the back of the wardrobe and find him.

There is no perfect place. Guys are everywhere. Yes, it's important that you choose wisely where you go when you go out, to maximize your opportunities to meet men, but the guys you eyeball at the Sapphire Room on Friday night will only ever represent a tiny proportion of the men you have the chance to meet during the rest of a normal week.

Don't wait for those occasional opportunities when you go to a party, or your night out with friends once a week. The truth is, Mr. Right does all of the things you do. He does not belong to a different species. Wherever you go, he goes. He is on the train, riding the escalator, shopping in the supermarket, relaxing in the coffee shop, playing sports, watching sports, in line at the movies, or at the cell phone store. He is everywhere.

As I sit here in a coffee shop writing this, I've noticed that three attractive women have walked in and ordered coffee. I could easily have been gazing at my computer screen wondering where all the great women are. Just because I didn't meet these women doesn't mean that they weren't there. The opportunities to meet people present themselves more often than we think.

While there is no perfect venue, some venues are better than others. You probably won't run across Mr. Right while getting your nails done; you have a better chance browsing at the Apple store. The best venue is rich in guys and allows for easy conversation. Your living room couch doesn't qualify.

One activity that could be made more sociable is the way we exercise. For example, if, when you're working out at the gym, you're used to cranking out hours on your own on the treadmill or exercise bike, try signing up for a class that's likely to be heavily male oriented, like kickboxing or martial arts.

This employs the concept of Double Time; without allocating any more time in your schedule, you've transformed a formerly solitary activity into one that is rich in guys and makes for easy conversation. Suddenly you've developed a ritual that takes no more time from your current schedule (since you would have been working out anyway) and gives you the chance to meet more guys.

Think about other ways you could put yourself in more sociable environments through exploring other interests, whether it's listening to live music in a jazz bar, taking a class in filmmaking, or joining a coed softball team. Do something you've always wanted to try but never have, like a wine tasting (or whiskey tasting if you want to make it even more guy heavy). I'm not suggesting you do something you're not into. Scuba certification courses are always guy heavy, but if you can't swim and hate the ocean, that isn't the place for you.

If nothing appeals to you at the moment and it all seems a bit overwhelming, just set up a new ritual of going out with friends two nights each week to places men frequent.

Also, finding guys in the course of your daytime activities is easier and more effective than at night. There is less pressure, and we don't usually expect a social exchange in the daytime.

Quick Ways to Build a Social Network

Having a vibrant circle of friends exponentially expands your chances of meeting new guys. The woman with a half dozen good pals not only has friends to hit the clubs with, or who'll join her on a river-rafting trip, she also knows six humans who have brothers, cousins, uncles, friends, coworkers, neighbors, and even ex-boyfriends.

To bring new people into your life:

Say yes

Parties, barbecues, dinners, theater trips—people are always inviting us to events, yet we often say no because we're too busy, we don't have the energy, or it's simply not our thing. Now, it's time for a new ritual: the one of saying yes.

Say yes to the colleague who invites you out for a drink after work. Say yes to baby showers, Super Bowl parties, and chili cook-offs. Most people are a little intimidated at the thought of going alone to that wedding or that birthday party of a friend of a friend, but from now on, if you've been invited, you're going to say yes. It's one of the oldest self-help clichés in the world, but to get different results we have to start doing things differently. Saying yes will open up your world and also give you a chance to exercise your social muscles.

Get good at WAR (working a room)

Building a social circle doesn't have to mean we go out every night of the week, but it does means we have to make our social time *quality* social time; it's not about the amount of time we have, it's about the intensity with which we use it. You've gone to the trouble of making yourself presentable and getting yourself to the function, so don't waste the evening by standing around staring at your phone.

What do most people do when they walk into a bar, party, or other social function? Flock to cover like mice. We immediately try to snag a table, or we take up residency in a corner of the room with our friends, or lean against a wall and madly start texting.

Next time you're tempted to do this, stop. When you enter a place, take it all in. Just stand for a second and take your time. Most people pace around so quickly because they're nervous. They're nervous to be in the middle of the room, and they get anxious about standing on their own. They have a difficult time confidently standing there. But just slow it down. Make some eye contact with people in the room.

Smile at them and allow everyone to notice you for a second. Don't try to quickly blend in to your surroundings or run to the shadows of the room.

"Working the room" may conjure up the image of the glad-handing politician trying to get votes, but I promise this has nothing to do with kissing strange babies and everything to do with simply connecting with others.

The secret is to start with frequent, small interactions with lots of different people. It's not about the length of the interaction, but the number.

Keep this initial interaction very simple. With some people just smile and say, "How are you doing tonight?" or, if you're at a friend's party, "How do you know Stephanie?" If you're getting a drink, you could just lean toward the guy next to you and ask, "What's the best cocktail on the menu here?" Talk to the bartender, even if you just ask him how he's doing.

Imagine you're just bouncing off people as you walk past them. Move through with confidence, keeping the conversation small, but aim to get their names. Before you leave a person, always ask, "What was your name again?" Make sure they know your name, and move on, saying something like "Have a great night."

WATCH MATT WORK A ROOM

Many people find working a room difficult. Watch me interact with audience members onstage so you can see this technique in action.

Go to **www.gettheguybook.com/war**
Access code: **gtgbook**

Adopt the ownership mentality

I remember arriving in New York the night before one of my Get the Guy seminars. I went down to the hotel bar for a drink. A guy came down the stairs, marched up to me, shook my hand, and with a big grin said, "Hey buddy, how's it going?" We spoke for no more than thirty seconds and then he left, saying, "Enjoy your night, I'll see you later." He didn't explain why he was speaking to me.

A few hours later I found out that this guy owned the bar. I didn't know that at first and just saw that he was open, warm, and friendly. I was receptive to him because he exuded charm and confidence. I could see him talking to everyone effortlessly. He was just a guy working the room.

The lesson was not lost on me. We can all adopt this mentality. Owners of establishments talk to anyone and everyone, even though many have no idea who they are, because, well, *they own the place*. But the reason behind their behavior hardly matters, because it's about the openness and warmth they project.

By adopting this attitude, a party that might seem intimidating when you walk in the door can feel in twenty minutes like one you're hosting. The best part? You're able to relax and feel at home without having to come up with anything clever or fancy to say.

Treat everyone the same

Being sociable is both learned behavior and an attitude. It doesn't have an on-off switch. Many people take a somewhat mercenary approach, as if their charm is a precious resource they'll run out of if they don't save it for the right time and person. "When I meet that amazing guy, *then* I'll bring out my full charm," they imagine. Or, at a party or event where there are no hot guys, they say things like, "I can't see anyone I'm attracted to here, so where's the benefit to me?" It's like saying, "When I get on the stage, then I'll learn my lines!"

Building a social network is not only about snagging a date with that one attractive guy. Nor is it about using people; our interest in them should always come from a genuine place.

Truth be told, I'm an introvert. My idea of a great evening is watching a movie at home with someone I care about, be it a girlfriend, family, or friends. Even so, I know that there are a lot of men and women out there who may introduce me to a lively social circle, or to new people and places. Some people may be more introspective but still have the potential of bringing something unexpected into our lives, even if it is an idea or point of view that we might not have otherwise come across. The point is that there is a great big world out there with your guy in it, and the only way to find him is to expand your world, even if it is one step at a time.

If you remain unconvinced about the benefits of saying yes, learning to work a room, and expanding your social network, consider this: being sociable is one of the key ways to throw the net wide: when we get sociable with *everyone*, it's easy to meet *anyone*. And by anyone I mean that hot guy you would normally pass by because you're too nervous to even make eye contact. You'll never know where Mr. Right will appear, and when he does it helps to be "in shape" socially, to be able to start a conversation, and get and keep him interested. (More about the latter, later.)

Be open to gateway friends

One time I was doing some coaching in central London, on Carnaby Street. Things were progressing well, or so I thought. Part of my method is to talk through a technique with a client, then encourage them to field test it by going out in the world and seeing for themselves how it works. One young woman had ventured out and struck up a conversation with a good-looking young guy, and from where I watched at my table outside a coffee shop, I could see them across the street having what appeared to be a great conversation. They were laughing over something she'd said, and I assumed they were having loads of fun. This was a date in the making for sure. She returned to where I was sitting, beaming.

"How did it go?" I asked.

"Great, he was really cool and interesting."

"Terrific," I said. "Did you get his number?"

"Oh no, I didn't really fancy him in that way, but he was great to talk to because he works in fashion, which is something I just love."

Where had I gone wrong? This was crazy! This guy was good-looking, cool, and seemed like he had a fascinating, glamorous life. She decided not to get his number because he wasn't her type.

Can you see why this is a problem? Whether she was attracted to him or not, how many *other* guys in central London might this guy know who are also cool, fashionable, and fun to be around? Who couldn't do with this kind of person in her contacts? Even if that particular guy wasn't my client's cup of tea, there's a chance that within his network there was a guy for her.

As soon as she closed off the opportunity to be in touch with that guy again, she lost not just him, but one, two, or maybe ten or more potential guys she could have been introduced to through this single gateway guy.

I'm not suggesting you lead a guy on when you're not interested. The object is to make a casual connection. My client could have easily said, "None of my friends have a clue about what's fashionable, you'd be performing a public service by letting me put you in my contacts."

The more playful and relaxed you make it, the less seriously he'll take it when you ask for the number. And with a gateway guy there's nothing to lose and everything to gain: you'll get to exercise your social muscles with a good-looking man, add to your social circle, and perhaps develop a friendship with the best friend of Mr. Right.

Meet people who share your passions

Earlier I discussed the benefits of pursuing your interests as a way of throwing the net wide and meeting more guys. You can also expand your social circle that way. When you sign up for that cooking class, it'll be full of people who share your passion for cooking. What kind of people are you going to meet at your one-day travel photography seminar? People who share the same interest.

The goal is not to fill your datebook with meaningless activities, but to enrich your life. The combination of saying yes to events and activities you might enjoy if you give them half a chance, plus enlarging your circle of friends and contacts, will result in a life you will love, and just may lead you to the love of your life.

Every Relationship Begins with a Conversation

It's not just where we go but what we do when we are there that counts. Exposing ourselves to opportunity is one thing, but it doesn't help if when we do go out we glue ourselves to one side of the room, clutching a drink, and get locked in conversation with the two friends we came with, only interrupting our conversation to check our phone. That evening will pass without our meeting anyone. So let's work on developing the ability to engage in high-quality social interactions— otherwise known as learning how to talk to people.

You may not think you are naturally sociable, but that is your perception, and because it's a perception not based in fact, it can be changed. You are human and therefore sociable. It is a species trait, not an individual one.

Being sociable has nothing to do with whether you're an introvert or an extrovert. Learning how to talk to people is about developing a skill, not changing who you are. Getting your guy doesn't require you to change anything about your character. It only requires you to do what human beings, as primates who live in groups composed of families, clans, and communities, do naturally: socialize. Being sociable is innate. This isn't about being the loudest, craziest person at the party, but being prepared to open up our world and show a genuine interest in other people. Every relationship begins with a conversation, *so you simply need to start having more of them.*

The act of starting a conversation may be the most important thing you do to get the guy. Starting conversations is so important that I can't stress it enough. Later on in the book we'll deal with the nitty-gritty of what to say to the guy you really like. For the moment, understand that what will transform your life, more than anything else, is to begin having more conversations.

People who are good at starting conversations aren't good because they have some magical method or great conversation pieces. They are good because they do it regularly, and the more they do it, the easier it gets. Even the simplest opening can start a conversation that can lead to something amazing.

You can ask your waiter what is the best thing on the menu. You can chat up the barman when ordering a drink. You can ask the woman standing online behind you at the grocery store her opinion on the organic peanut butter she's got in her cart.

A lot of conversations go nowhere. That's the nature of interactions. Just because you've asked someone the time doesn't mean you're going to wind up standing on the street corner discussing the state of the global economy for an hour. Sometimes you'll have a two-minute chat, share a silly joke, then both be on your way. That's okay, as your focus should be on the process and your comfort in it.

It's fun to make someone smile by offering a compliment, or asking their advice, or displaying interest in a book they might be reading. People, no matter who they are, feel good about themselves when someone notices them.

If the thought of this makes you nervous, chances are it's because you're still imagining that the only new people you're going to chat up in any given week are guys to whom you're attracted. There's one in line at the deli! Oh my God, how can I approach him, and what do I say when I do? He's going to think I'm a crazy person!

If you focus solely on the conversations you're going to initiate with men you find attractive, you will not get good at this. People who are the most magnetic are people who are able to meet anyone, who can relate to or charm everyone, whether male or female. They're not thinking about being humiliated or embarrassed or rejected, because their intent is just to be sociable.

If you become the kind of person who's always able to start a conversation and connect with people, when you do meet that hot guy you'll be less likely to get tongue-tied, because you'll have well-exercised social muscles. Conversation will feel natural and easy, because it's become a ritual.

When we just focus on practicing conversation for its own sake, we stop fearing the outcome, because each conversation just makes us better prepared for the next one.

Be a Tourist

One of my favorite ways of making conversation easy is to imagine you are a tourist. Wherever you live, imagine you've just arrived in town. What does that mindset feel like? You're alert and full of questions. Your curiosity (and interest in where the nearest bathroom is) probably makes you more bold than usual. Tourists often say about London or New York, "Everyone here is just so friendly when you speak to them." Londoners and New Yorkers often feel just the opposite.

The difference is the tourist mindset. Tourists walk around inquisitively. They ask directions, they talk to locals when they meet them, they ask random people about the area, and often they get chatty when they go out because they want to meet people. Because of this everyone in the city seems friendly and responds to them by being warm and open. Tourists, unlike most locals, treat the city as a playground where they can meet anybody.

Not long ago I was in a supermarket in London with my brother. It was early Saturday morning and we'd stumbled out in our pajamas, hoping to grab something for breakfast. Two American girls approached us and said, "Do you know anywhere good for breakfast around here? We just got here yesterday and don't really know the area."

"I know some great places," I said, and told them what they were. Then I said, "You guys seem really cool. We should get some of our friends together and go out sometime."

It was so simple and obvious, and we ended the conversation exchanging numbers. The reason this worked so well is that the girls put zero pressure on the interaction. They were seeking information and took a chance that two moderately hungover guys in their pajamas could help them out.

You can do this right now. You don't have to wait until you are a tourist in a new city. Be a tourist in your own town. Who can honestly say they've explored everywhere in the town that they live? Once you just get curious about people and places, you lose all that anxiety about approaching people. You lose that ridiculous idea that every interaction has two possible outcomes: approval or rejection.

Instead, you're out there living life, meeting people, enlarging your circle of friends, until one day, you meet a guy who's worth getting to know.

4

===

The Mindset of the Chooser

Among the misconceptions perpetrated about men and what they think, the biggest is this:

"If he really liked me he would come over and talk to me."

No, he wouldn't.

I have coached over ten thousand guys, and if I've learned anything, it's that when it comes to striking up a conversation, whether a guy likes you is absolutely irrelevant. He could be standing right next to you, thinking you're a goddess and the girl of his dreams, and he might not do a thing about it.

In fact, the more attracted to you a guy is, the less likely he is to approach you. Why? Because it's easier for him to talk to a woman he doesn't like. Talking to the girl who makes him melt inside is hard as hell.

Those who subscribe to the hard-to-get school of courtship contend that a woman should always wait for a guy to approach her, because then, and only then, can she tell whether a guy is actually into her or not.

I'm here to break the news: there isn't an ounce of truth in this.

Blame TV, blame the movies, but there's an enormous fallacy that men approach women on a regular basis. It is a mistaken belief that men are the ones who initiate contact, that a girl simply has to show up, and the guys who are drawn to her will behave like bees around a flower.

If your experience bears this out—that men don't approach you regularly—you're probably convinced that this means you're not attractive to men.

The reality is that most men are not used to approaching women they're drawn to. Whether he's a Calvin Klein underwear model or the most average-looking guy on the street, most men do not approach women on a regular basis. I know dozens of guys who are good-looking and charming, smart and accomplished, or warm and funny, who never approach women when they go out. That is, of course, unless they are plied with alcohol or the woman in question is their best friend's friend.

This is not to say that no men ever approach women. But most of those who do tend to approach a lot of women. Hitting on women is their go-to social move. I don't have a national polling organization on my payroll, but I'd wager that these outgoing, hey-babe-buy-you-a-drink? guys make up 1 percent of the population. Chances are, if a guy sidles up to you at a party and is laying it on heavy, he is a guy you may want to avoid. While this is happening, all around you are a bunch of worthy, intriguing guys who are not in the habit of speaking to women they don't know. Even if these guys somehow believe it's their social, chivalric duty to do the approaching, they're just not very good at it. Unless they get some help or buy a book like this one, they're even less accomplished at it than you are.

The scene is familiar. It's your friend's birthday party. Or maybe she's not really a friend, she's just sort of someone you know. You're surprised she invited you, but a few of your friends convinced you to go. Now you're at the party, the friends who dragged you here have wandered off, and you're clutching a drink.

You spot a cute guy at the other side of the room. You think he's looking over at you. Wouldn't it be really great if he came over for a chat? He looks over. He just smiled. You notice that he looks even cuter when he smiles. You smile back. Why doesn't he just come over?

It's okay, you think. Someone will probably introduce you both later. He probably knows one of your friends. Or maybe the host will introduce you. You carry on with your night, catching up with the few people you know in the room. He smiles again. Then he takes his drink and starts to move off. He gives you a lingering look before joining a group of his friends.

Maybe you feel a familiar sense of frustration. Why didn't he come over and say hello?

What Freaks Guys Out About Approaching a Woman

Try putting yourself in the shoes of a guy for a second. Suppose he spots you from the other side of the room, and he's decided he likes what he sees. He now has a decision to make: Should he walk across the room and strike up a conversation with you or not? And if not, why not? What's he got to worry about?

He's worried about looking bad in front of his friends

Looking like an idiot in front of his friends means far more to a guy than a girl can ever imagine. What if he strolls over to you and you shoot him down, or give him the blank look of death? What if he thinks your boyfriend is about to return from the bar with a handsome martini? He'll be left to do one thing: walk s-l-o-w-l-y back to his friends, who will rib him and laugh at him, thereby lowering his self-esteem and guaranteeing that he never initiates another conversation with a female for as long as he lives. These fears are so primal and embedded in the male psyche that even if you give him signals to approach you, he may still misread them.

To fail with the opposite sex is a huge blow to the male ego, bigger than any woman can ever imagine. This fear of humiliation is what fuels the male impulse to fabricate fantasy hookups, and why guys who *never* get laid still brag to their friends that they do. It's why younger men have bragging competitions about the women they have slept with, or the hot model who gave them her phone number, or the number of dates they've been on in the last week.

It's the desire for sexual validation that explains male posturing, posing, and the kind of one-upmanship that dominates so much masculine behavior. Ever notice how male bonding tends to be centered around putting each other down and making each other look stupid? Friendships between men are still often built on fighting for status.

What's more, a man fights hardest for social status among his own peers. The men whose opinions he cares the most about are *not* all the strangers in the bar, but his friends. It's within his own group he has to fight for dominance, which is why any public humiliation, particularly humiliation from women, is so painful.

He's terrified of what you and your friends are going to say

The risk of rejection by you, and the ridicule he imagines he'll then suffer at the hands of your friends, is excruciating—so much so that he would rather hang back and at least cling to the belief that he *could* approach you, if he so desired, than risk the prospect of rejection. If you see him talking to other women, chances are it's because he feels he has absolutely nothing to lose.

When it comes to your average man, it's precisely the woman who drives him crazy who seems the *most* terrifying to him. He feels unworthy of her. He feels that she has her pick of any guy in the place.

Also, his status as a man is on the line, so if he approaches her and gets shot down, he's going to feel that sting of rejection that we all instinctively try to avoid.

In this way, men and women aren't that different. You probably feel just as nervous around a guy you think is hot as a guy does around a woman to whom he's attracted. Think how much easier it is to flirt and act sexy with a guy you're not interested in: it's the same for us.

Why is this? I could ask you to approach a stranger and ask him for the time, and you wouldn't feel nervous. You might feel a little awkward at first, but you wouldn't feel any actual pressure. Even if I asked you to approach the most attractive person in the room to ask where the restroom was located, it might not be that intimidating.

What's the crucial distinction between approaching someone for directions and approaching a potential love interest for conversation?

It's all in your intent.

Our intentions are responsible for making us nervous.

When we approach someone to ask for the time, we have no ulterior motive. We are seeking information, plain and simple. It's straightforward. It's not about *who* we ask, not about any person in particular.

But the instant you think, "I'm approaching him because I would like to get his phone number, which I hope will lead to a date," you seize up, because there's always the possibility he'll reject you. It's your intent that creates pressure on a simple social interaction. Your intent fuels feelings of nervousness and anxiety.

Because your intent exposes your most vulnerable hopes and desires—he's hot! I want him to like-maybe-love me!—you fall into the mindset that you'll either be Accepted or Rejected. The stakes are suddenly high. This is now serious business. You worry (even obsess) about the way he is going to react to you. Why? Because now you're desperate for his approval.

It's not unlike the nervousness we experience in a job interview.

When we're sitting around with our friends it's easy to talk about our qualities and what makes us an ideal candidate, but when we're sitting across from the person who has it in their power to hire us, we're ill at ease, because we're attached to the outcome.

The very moment you're invested in a guy's approval is the same moment all of those traits that make you a vibrant, spontaneous, intriguing, sexually attractive woman mysteriously vanish.

The Conundrum

I'm sure you're ahead of me here. If guys won't make the first move, and if you, as a high-value woman, aren't about to chase after them, how does anyone ever meet anyone? Furthermore, men like to feel as if they've done something special to earn your attraction; the more you seem to be "chasing" a guy, the less interested he is. No matter how far we've come socially, a stubborn prevailing idea persists of how boy meets girl: that it is the man's role to be the pursuer and the women's job to either accept or reject him.

My friend Jenny was completely fed up. We were meeting in a coffee shop, but she was in no mood for small talk. "All the guys who approach me are just complete idiots who I have no interest in. All the guys I approach won't give me the time of day. There's just no one out there—it's hopeless."

"So, what now?" I asked. "Do you think there are *any* men in the world who would live up to your standards?"

"There must be. I just don't know how to meet them."

Jenny was stuck. She had specific ideas about how meeting a guy should be: "I don't want to look desperate. It's the guy's job to do the work. I'm not going to go around like some predatory woman trying to track down men. It's not feminine."

Jenny's concerns are legitimate. No woman wants to look desperate or feel as if she's doing all the work. No woman wants to feel as if she had to track down Prince Charming like a lioness hunting her prey.

We're still living in an era when dating advice generally holds that it's a woman's obligation to be chased, that her role in the courtship process is to wait for a man to approach, since anything else will only make her appear desperate and needy. Let's dispense with this false wisdom right now. We've already talked about the pitfalls of waiting. Now it's time to talk about the creating part, and how you can do this without compromising your sense of being of high value.

Two Ways to Eliminate Your Anxiety About Making the First Move

What if there was a way to make the first move without jeopardizing all of those attractive qualities you have now so beautifully cultivated? Let's put you in control so you can choose the men who will approach you. Yes, in this case, you can have your cake and eat it, too. I am going to tell you how.

Change your intent

A few pages back we talked about how intent can cause us to fumble if it pertains to something for which we have a vested interest in the outcome. Most of us treat talking to an attractive stranger as though it's the final heat of an Olympic event. We behave as though we have one chance to win, and if we fail it's over. We'll have to wait another four years to get another shot at the gold, and by then we might be too old. Instead of approaching a guy with the intention that he might be The One, do it with the notion that you will never see or talk to him again. Just think about how freeing that would be. If your intention is only to engage for one moment and move on, then there is less at stake. It's like running a race: you focus on getting to the next marker, not the finish line, and that gets you, invariably, to the finish line!

The truth is, you get as many chances to approach guys as you want. If one encounter doesn't work out, you can move on and engage with someone new. You couldn't speak to a tenth of the interesting people on this earth even if you went from guy to guy to guy 24-7 for the rest of your life. The opportunities are limitless—remember our theory of abundance versus scarcity. There's an old saying that men are like buses: if you miss one, there's always another coming along in a few minutes. The sooner you embrace this truth, the sooner you can get on with meeting your one and only.

Place less value on the outcome

Whenever we're worried about someone else's reaction to us, it's a sign that we're placing too much value on their opinion. And why do we care about their opinion? Because we're still too invested in the outcome.

Rejection is not the worst experience in life. We humans are amazingly resilient. For one thing, the biological imperative to procreate hardwires us to keep at it until we've found a mate. The species would have died out long ago if we gave up after one rejection. Besides, when we bounce back from failure we become more confident. It is certainly better to deal with rejection than to realize too late that we never ventured out and got what we wanted because we were too worried about what people thought about us. Remember, the pain of rejection is nothing compared to the pain of regret.

To put this in perspective: Why should you get nervous at the idea of starting a conversation with someone you find attractive when you don't know a single thing about him? Right now, he's just a smile, some hair, a shirt that brings out the blue of his eyes. That's it, nothing more. You don't even know this person. Why place so much importance on what he thinks of you? Try to think about it this way: he has to *earn* an opinion about you. That's why you are talking to him. Everything else is nonsense.

You'll Never Be Everyone's Cup of Tea

Even if you change your intent, place less value on the outcome, adopt the mindset of the chooser, and wear your lucky shoes, there will always be conversations that won't go as you'd like them to.

And that's okay. Sometimes the guy you're interested in will give you the cold shoulder, or be into someone else. For all you know, he might be gay or already in a relationship. It doesn't matter. It only matters that you tried. That's the success story here.

Whether you're trying to get the guy or just get through the day, rejection is inevitable. There will always be people with whom you don't connect. When we're applying for a job and send out twenty résumés, most of us expect that at least half of those will be rejections because the fit isn't right. It doesn't reflect on our worth as a person. The same holds true when you're approaching men who look interesting. You'll win some, you'll lose some. As a friend who's a doctor points out, "Statistics never matter to the individual." There could be a one-in-a-thousand chance you're going to come down with some disease, but if you're that one, the stats go out the window. Likewise, for our purposes, it doesn't matter how many divorces there are, or what the ratio of single men to single women is, or how many times you get rejected. You only need to find your ideal partner once. And once you do, every statistic will be irrelevant.

The Odds Are Better Than You Think

Many women worry that there's too much competition out there. If you find yourself falling into this trap I want to remind you of something: most women aren't doing anything to find the guy, so they're not competing with you. They are either hanging out at home on their Facebook page or out with their friends talking about how there are no guys out there.

On my weekend seminar my clients go out on Saturday night and practice what they learned that day. One of my clients told me about a group of beautiful women who sat at a nearby table and no one approached them all evening, while my clients had engaged almost every guy in the venue.

This was a lesson I learned at my first school dance. The girls stood on one side, the guys on the other. Then I noticed one guy getting all the attention—he was simply the guy who had crossed the room. I remember thinking when I got home, I can't believe how much I missed by focusing on competition that wasn't even there!

How to Overcome Your Fear of Hot Guys

It's normal to feel a few butterflies in your stomach when you're approaching a guy you find attractive or compelling, but if you're nervous to the point of speechlessness, it's important to ask yourself this two-part question: What are you overvaluing about him at that moment? And, more important, what are you undervaluing about yourself?

Remind yourself how high your standards are for a relationship. Think about the list of qualities your ideal man must possess. He must be kind, generous, challenging, ambitious, caring, optimistic, intelligent, polite, amiable with your friends, playful, adventurous, physically appealing, and a hundred other qualities.

This list should remind you that you are extremely fussy. Not any guy will fit the bill. In fact, *most* guys won't fit the bill.

His good looks tell you nothing except for the first flush of, oh yes, *him*, I'd like to talk to him. But good looks are just one of dozens of qualities you require. His score is one out of twenty, and it might end right there. Talking to him is a method of discovering how many other attributes on your list he might possess. This isn't about being arrogant or judgmental, it's about taking a long step back and putting appearance in its proper place.

What if you learned that the hot guy over by the punch bowl who's making your palms sweat and your stomach flip-flop was cold, selfish, dull, and had a criminal record for beating up his previous girlfriends? Would you still turn to jelly at the thought of talking to him? As a friend who's completely conquered her fear of talking to attractive men likes to remind herself if she starts feeling nervous, "Ted Bundy was great looking, and he turned out to be a serial killer."

Yet, when we see someone whose looks we like and we feel that rush of attraction, we project every good quality we desire onto them, even though we have absolutely no basis for doing so.

He's just a guy you want to talk to—nothing more.

Whenever you find yourself feeling intimidated at the prospect of starting a conversation, remind yourself, This guy has a lot to prove before he lives up to my standards.

Whenever you make an effort to speak to a guy, it's because you're merely curious. It's not because you want him. You are just giving him the opportunity to impress you. You're giving him a chance to prove his personality can match up to his initial attractiveness.

Thinking this way begins to put you in the mindset of the chooser.

———

When I auditioned for NBC's reality matchmaking show *Ready for Love*, I flew to LA for a screen test. The people at the network made it clear that my being cast in the show would depend on how I did in front of the camera. I was nervous as hell. The day of my flight, I received a brilliant e-mail from my friend Jon Turteltaub, a film director, who offered some great wisdom:

> *Think of this screen test the same way you would think about approaching a woman. If you focus on the fact that you desperately need something from her, you'll be insecure and awkward. If you focus on the fact that you're already desired because you're already charming, smart, funny, and knowledgeable, then you'll be confident and charismatic.*
>
> *You also never get a girl by acting competitive with other guys. Just be the best version of yourself, and if the chemistry is right . . . and the girl is smart and astute . . . she'll choose you. This is as easy as can be.*
>
> *Oh, one more thing . . . wear an antiperspirant and your lucky shoes.*

I took his advice and got the job. And I've worn antiperspirant ever since.

5

The Traits of Desirable Women

When I was a kid growing up in Essex, England, my dad owned a nightclub, and the club had a DJ. I must have been about eleven when I got it into my head that I wanted to be a DJ too. I went out and bought a pair of turntables and two or three vinyl albums, and I started practicing in my bedroom.

My dad is an entrepreneurial sort. Even though he had a lot of successful ventures, and there were times when we lived in a big house, there were also times when things weren't going so well, financially, and we lived in a trailer. But my dad loved books and learning, and no matter where we lived we always had books.

One day I was looking around on the bookshelf and came across *How to Win Friends and Influence People*. I remember thinking how tragic my life would have to be that I would need to *win* friends. But I picked it up anyway, and after about ten pages I was hooked.

I was floored by the notion that there were behaviors that you could learn that had nothing to do with your looks, your education, or your background; that there was a formula and a set of tools that could get you further with people. I felt like I was learning a superpower, and I started to apply the principles in the book to my DJ aspirations.

I realized that the difference between people who get ahead in life is not talent, necessarily, but knowing the right people and knowing how to be around them. I knew of a lot of great DJs who were exceptional but were working for public radio stations for free. I also knew of DJs who were just okay but were getting a thousand bucks a night just because they were friendly with the owner of a good club. I realized that I could practice DJing in my bedroom for the next ten years, but if I didn't know how to talk to people, how to "win friends," there was a good chance I'd never get anywhere. I started to talk about myself as a DJ at school. I didn't say I wanted to be one, or that I was practicing to be one, I just said I was one. To my amazement, my classmates just accepted it. Word got around, and one day an upperclassman asked me to DJ at a party he was throwing.

I said I'd love to, even though I was twelve years old and I had no idea how to get my stuff to the party. But it was a great opportunity and I did it for nothing. And word continued to spread.

Four parties later, someone offered me fifty pounds to do a party and that became my going rate. Until I started charging a hundred, then three hundred, and so on. And my reputation grew around Essex, until everyone who threw a party with a DJ had decided I was the DJ to get.

Charming, you may be thinking, but what's that got to do with me?

Earlier in this book, I listed the attributes of the woman of high value. She is certain and confident about her own worth. She is independent, and has a life that she loves that any guy would be thrilled to be a part of. She has principles and the integrity to uphold them. She is not afraid to be feminine.

All of this is well and good, but it's not unlike me practicing my mad DJing skills in my bedroom. Until I became a DJ in the eyes of others, nothing happened. So I started calling myself a DJ and behaving like a DJ, and eventually people accepted me as one. Likewise, to get the guy it's not enough to *be* a woman of high value, the men you meet have to *know* that you are someone special. When a guy realizes you're not just any girl, but one of high value, you become something else in his eyes: a desirable woman.

You Sexy Thing

Sex is such a defining part of a relationship that it's important to express your sexuality in the early stages. Sexuality doesn't mean coming on to every guy who makes eye contact. Indeed, women who try to play on their sexuality too quickly can make a man feel either suspicious or threatened.

A desirable woman doesn't disguise her ability to be comfortable with her sexual self, and she is able to express it. This expression can, and perhaps should, be subtle. You express your sexuality in the way you move, in your willingness to throw a seductive look out now and then, in being able to playfully touch a guy with confidence.

It's also about being comfortable with allowing an atmosphere of sexual tension. Women who aren't comfortable with this will often deflect a man's affections and immediately change the subject when he tries to communicate *his* sexual desire. Sometimes she'll deflate the tension by closing down when the conversation veers into more intimate territory. This is fine if you are not interested in pursuing something more with him. If you are interested, it can stop the momentum cold.

Never underestimate the power of embracing and expressing your sexuality. Many a man has snagged a date with a so-called gorgeous woman, only to find that she's cold and remote. She may be objectively beautiful in the eyes of the world, but without the ability to express her sexual nature, she'll never be able to make a man feel a strong physical desire for her.

All men have had this experience: they meet someone they find beautiful, but then in conversation she's a hollow shell. She might be friendly and pleasant enough to talk to, but just connecting isn't flirting. Flirting is what puts someone on our radar. Without flirting, a date is just two people having a conversation. When there's sexual energy on a date, a man shouldn't be able to stop thinking about kissing you.

Playfulness, the essential ingredient

Women are close to ruling the universe these days. At most of my Get the Guy Women's Weekends, I meet CEOs, small-business owners, lawyers, doctors, consultants of every stripe. They consider themselves to be of high value in part because they're used to marching out into the world, kicking ass, and getting what they want. They're used to being in control.

Whenever I discuss traits like certainty, they nod in agreement. They have no problem being certain. They may be responsible for a large team of subordinates who rely on them to keep it together. Sometimes they have to be aggressive to get that client, or to make that deal, or to stay above the competition. They are used to networking, meeting, charming, and doing business with people they don't know.

When I begin talking about what makes someone appealing in conversation, someone will eventually become impatient and say, "I do this every day. I know how to meet people and be charming in conversation. I have no problem working a room and being confident. I'm in charge of a huge sales team of men and have no problem being the leader in a social situation. Enough of this confidence stuff, just give me the formula for attraction and I'll do it. Confidence isn't my problem."

But confidence isn't transferable across all areas of our lives. Although we may feel certain and confident in one aspect of our lives, it doesn't mean that we automatically do in others.

On the Saturday night of every coaching program, the women I coach go out to put their newfound knowledge to the test. At a recent event I suggested to Diana, one of the attendees, who'd described herself as "very confident" earlier in the day, that she go over and talk to a guy having a drink at the bar.

The expression on Diana's face changed in an instant. "I don't know. He's just standing there, I can't just walk up to him."

"Would you be able to approach him if you were at a networking event?" I asked.

"Sure. I'm just not used to approaching them in this way. At a business event I could do it with no problem."

Suddenly, now that the conversation isn't about networking, the whole idea produces a feeling of terror. Diana's intent changed—instead of making a business contact, she was attempting to make a personal one, and she felt completely out of her element. She couldn't ask for his number under the pretext of exchanging business cards, so her confidence drained away. This isn't to say that Diana is not a confident person; she just isn't confident *in this situation*.

Of course she could have just dialed in her business mode, ask the guy what he did for a living, and talk about what she does for work. This is the kind of conversation with which she is most comfortable, and isn't it better to be comfortable and confident than the deer in the headlights?

Not at all.

Because Diana's goal here was to create interest and attraction, which requires displaying a different side of her personality, one that is playful.

Playfulness is the essential ingredient in conveying your desirability. Confidence and certainty form the foundation of interactions, but a woman's ability to drop her professional persona and have fun helps creates spark in the conversation. A professional woman used to meeting men has perfected a persona that is all business. She knows she can speak with a guy for hours without creating any chemistry or attraction—which likely serves her well in the business environment.

The inability or disinclination to tap into one's playful side isn't exclusive to women. Men also face this problem when they try to adopt what I like to call the James Bond persona. A guy donning the full James Bond persona puts on his serious face, leans on the bar, and tries to look stern and mysterious while sipping his martini. In reality, he just appears moody and standoffish (or idiotic, if he takes it too far).

To be playful is to take yourself, and all your interactions, less seriously. Adding a hint of playfulness into your conversations with guys is how you create chemistry. The ability to joke around, tease, tell funny stories, and be silly makes us more attractive and charismatic.

Spontaneity

Contrary to popular belief, spontaneity isn't about being the kooky girl who lives a crazy, off-the-wall lifestyle and jets off on random island adventures at the drop of a hat. (Although, as I write this, that doesn't sound too bad.)

For our purposes, spontaneity means being able to be in the moment. It's about getting out of our heads, ditching our well-laid plans, and allowing the conversation to go where it will.

Good conversations never follow a logical progression. Think about a typical conversation with your best friend. Rarely will it ever involve a boring exchange of information, in which you both recite exactly what you've been up to over the last week, from start to finish. More likely, the conversation jumps all over the place. One minute you'll be talking about your day, and then you'll jump to "Oh my god, I have to tell you this story about this guy I met." Before you know it you'll be talking about a movie you saw recently, and then you'll immediately change the subject to family, then comment on her new shoes, and on and on it goes. This is because you are comfortable with this person. The unexpected, spontaneous nature of this kind of conversation is what makes it interesting and engaging.

Imagine if you could re-create this kind of give-and-take in any social environment. What if you could cut through all of the getting-to-know-you crap and get straight into being comfortable with a stranger within the first ten minutes?

Being spontaneous allows for this. The irony of trying to become acquainted with someone new is that we ask them exactly the kinds of questions that tell us nothing about who they are. Ten minutes talking about a guy's favorite movie is a better way to tap into any chemistry you may share than an hour spent exchanging your regular résumé-type information of where you work and what you do there.

Consider the conversational habits of kids. They're nothing but spontaneous. A child can be sitting drawing a picture of a house, then turn and ask "Do you like *Star Wars*?" or "Which superhero would you want to be?" She doesn't care if it's relevant or not, it was a question that came to mind.

In the first minute of conversation, if you ask a guy something like, "If you were to ditch work tomorrow and could do anything in the world, what would you do?" you'll have a better shot at a stimulating conversation than if you had spent a whole hour talking about what you both do for a living.

The beauty of this is that because it's a playful, spontaneous-seeming question, most guys will be caught off guard and are likely to answer honestly.

If he says, "I guess I would fly to Paris and have lunch in the Eiffel Tower," you can shoot back with a playful "Hmm, I was thinking a beach break in Hawaii. Are you more of a city guy or a sun-and-sand guy?"

Not only is this more interesting than asking what he does as assistant to the assistant vice president at Dewey, Cheatham, and Howe, it also allows both of you to display your personalities. The guy will instantly associate you with adventure and fun, and see your playful side within the first few minutes of your interaction. You are also jarring him out of his normal pattern of conditioned responses, and therefore making him reveal things to you he doesn't normally talk about with others. Spontaneity, because it traffics in the unexpected, gives a guy the sense that there's more to learn about you. Guys are intrigued by the idea that there are different sides to you, and if they hang around, they'll get a chance to see them. They want to feel like the longer they stick around, the more interesting things are going to get.

Cultivate Traits of the High-Value and Desirable Woman

The list of traits in this chapter and chapter 2 may sound a bit daunting, but everyone possesses them to varying degrees. Think of them as different muscles that may need to be trained. A woman may be close to everything a man wants, but he can't see himself with her because she never shows him she's sexual. Or, she seems so sexy and intelligent, but she's never playful and fun, so he can't picture himself just hanging out and joking around with her.

The reason a guy gets hooked on one woman is not because she is *just* sexy, or *just* playful, or *just* certain, or *just* feminine, or *just* bursting with integrity, but because she possesses a unique combination of traits: the girl who is warm, has integrity, and can charm his family, then rips his clothes off in the bedroom and is a sexual goddess; the girl who is playful with his friends, can debate politics like a pro, but knows how to enjoy a lazy Sunday watching movies and eating pizza; the girl who is independent, kicks ass out in the world, but is feminine and loving with her man.

Women like this cause an alarm to go off inside a guy's head and heart. Keep her, he thinks. This one's amazing! The longer he's around you, the more he believes you're not like anyone else and that he couldn't find what you have to offer in any other woman. You become irreplaceable.

This explains why a guy who seems only a little interested at first becomes more deeply attached the more time he spends with you. Or a guy who says, and even thinks, he's dating around, playing the field, enjoying the single life, and then suddenly meets a woman who possesses a unique combination of these traits and *wow!* He doesn't want to date anyone else.

I know this sounds like men want it all. They do.

But so do you!

You want the gentleman with the edge. You want the sensitive guy with the adventurous streak. The intellectual who is also amazing in bed. The charismatic popular guy who is also cultured and has deep values. When someone possesses a unique combination of traits, they become special in our eyes, and we want to hold on to them.

6

===

The White Handkerchief Approach

In Victorian society, it was generally forbidden for a woman to overtly pursue a man she found interesting. The total value of a woman in this era, the only thing that made her seem desirable, was the degree to which she was pursued. If she were seen to be actively chasing a man, it would probably lower her value in his eyes, and in the eyes of her family and society.

Even though they were hobbled by these strict rules, women still found a way to approach a man they desired.

If a woman was out for a stroll and spied a man she'd like to get to know better, she would drop her handkerchief as she passed by, then continue walking. The gallant hero, taking note of the handkerchief that had fallen to the ground in his path, would pick up the hand-kerchief and run after the lady to return the item to her, demonstrating that he was indeed a chivalrous, kind, and considerate gentleman. This also provided him with the chance to open a conversation with her, beginning with, "You dropped this, madam?"

This would allow the gallant hero to believe that fate had conspired with Cupid, dropping the white handkerchief of the perfect woman directly in his path. Of course, the woman would know the truth, that she had orchestrated the entire interaction.

She chose him and she made the first move. But it was subtle, simple, and elegant. It was a first move in disguise. Nothing that happened afterward would have taken place had she not dropped her handkerchief.

Obviously, women don't carry white handkerchiefs as a matter of course anymore, but that's no reason to ditch what is fundamentally a genius approach to getting a guy to initiate a conversation. As we know, most guys won't come over and say hello of their own accord. This doesn't mean they're not looking for an excuse to come over. That's all the white handkerchief approach is at bottom—a way of signaling to a guy you've selected that he can speak to you without fear of being rejected.

The Modern-Day White Handkerchief Approach

My new, retooled version for the twenty-first century solves the conundrum of how a high-value woman can initiate contact with the guy of her choice without chasing him. At the same time, it permits the guy to feel it is hc who has boldly taken advantage of an opportunity that fate has put in his path.

The look

Most people have an undeservedly high opinion of their ability to get the most out of eye contact. I've witnessed dozens of women during my weekend seminars sit in a pub, flash a guy a split-second look from the corner of their eye, then spin back around to their friends and say, "Okay, he knows I've seen him. If he doesn't come over now then he's not interested."

Meanwhile, the guy is oblivious. Anyone, aside from the woman who threw him a millisecond glance that even the Flash would miss, could see that the guy had no clue that anything had transpired, much less a woman conveying her interest in him.

My experience has been that what you may think is a blatant signal, a guy will interpret as you looking for the whereabouts of the bartender or the bathroom. Just looking in his general direction doesn't count as a "look."

Men are not good at picking up on body language cues. Psychological studies repeatedly tell us that the average woman is far more capable than the average man of interpreting nonverbal cues. This means that when it comes to us guys, you've got to lay it on thicker than you think is necessary. Often we really are as clueless as you suppose we are.

As a rule, women always overestimate the confidence of men. He's not James Bond (even if he is trying to work the Bond persona); he's just some guy hoping to get through the evening without looking like an idiot. Most guys are not confident enough to come over on the off chance that your quick glance was for them and not the waiter.

To get a guy's attention might require you to give a guy *two* looks.

Give him one half-second look, a brief turn of your head and a flash of eye contact to encourage him to notice you, then turn back to your friends (your book, your phone, your gin and tonic). This look is not meant to convey anything other than that you've noted his existence. For all he knows, you're looking to see where your boyfriend is.

The second look is going to convey the simple message *yes, I saw you and I'm curious.* To convey this message, the second look needs to offer a bit of character, nothing wild or elaborate. Just a slight smile, perhaps a cheeky look over the shoulder. You are turning only your head toward him, not your whole body.

In a study conducted at the University of Wisconsin examining the role of social cues in human interactions, it was found that a smile made a man 70 percent more likely to approach a woman than eye contact alone.

We hardly ever smile at someone, even someone we want to meet.

People find this hard to believe at first. Because we equate smiling with being nice, and because most of us believe that we're pretty nice, we believe we smile more than we actually do. The next time you go to the supermarket, count the number of times you catch someone's eye but don't smile. Once you become aware of this, you will find that you can catch yourself not smiling at people all day long. As we go through our days, most of us wear what I like to call screensaver face. We present our screensaver face even to people we like.

I realize that you may struggle with shyness, but remember: the smallest changes in our daily rituals can yield huge results.

A woman named Julia, who attended one of my weekend seminars, had always been terrified of holding eye contact for too long. She was extraordinarily worried about giving the wrong impression. She feared that even if she looked in a guy's direction she would come off as too aggressive.

She didn't believe that the reason guys weren't approaching her was that she couldn't bring herself to make eye contact. She believed there must be a bigger, unfixable reason: men could sense something deeply unsexy about her personality, or she was destined never to be the kind of girl that a guy would pick out of a crowd.

She never met anyone, much less dated. She was so depressed about the state of her love life, she realized she had nothing to lose. She made a resolution to do what she could to be more approachable.

One day she was sitting in the café at the gym doing some work on her laptop. She spotted a cute personal trainer who she'd noticed a few times before when she was running on the treadmill. The only attention he'd paid her was holding the door open for her a couple of times. But this day was going to be different. She was going to be Approachable Julia now.

She called over one of the female instructors; she knew that if she could be friendly and have a laugh with her, she would seem easier for anyone to approach. While Julia and the female instructor were chatting, she snuck a look at the guy. He didn't come over, but she seemed to have caught his attention because he kept looking over while he was ordering some food from the café.

The female instructor left, and Julia sat alone at her table pretending to play with her laptop, a girl's best prop when she needs to look busy. She saw him out the corner of her eye, looked up, made quick eye contact, then lost her nerve. She dropped her gaze, trying her best to appear fascinated by the computer screen.

Come on, she thought, I have to do better than that. Just 1 percent more. She could feel the moment slipping away. This guy had shown signs of interest and here she was, again, wimping out. She could feel him looking over at her.

Screw it! She couldn't leave that gym and feel like a failure again. Without thinking, she looked up, held her eyes on his. Everything in that moment made her want to break eye contact and look away, but she let herself relax into it. It started to feel okay. Nothing bad was happening here. She felt so pleased with herself that she allowed a cheeky grin to creep onto her face. Julia knew other people would think she was being silly, but it was a big deal for her to hold eye contact for that extra second. She could feel her cheeks flush red from nerves.

But it paid off. He smiled back. They smiled at each other for a few seconds. Then he mouthed the word "Hey."

The trainer picked up his lunch and moved to the table next to her. She pretended to be working on her laptop, when all of a sudden he leaned over and said, "You look creative."

It was a strange line, but what the hell! They chatted for about twenty minutes. Near the end of their conversation, Julia felt her shyness creeping back. She closed her laptop, made some excuses, and left before they could exchange details or agree to meet later, but next time she saw him in the gym he made a point of saying, "I haven't seen you for ages."

Nothing has happened with the trainer—yet—but Julia has begun to practice making eye contact and smiling with guys she sees as she goes about her daily life, and enjoys the fact that for the most part, they're smiling back. The best part, she told me, is that she now feels such a sense of possibility and hope for the future. If nothing else, the small exchanges make for a much more pleasant day.

One of my main tenets is that if you're *always* ready to meet a guy, you never have to *get* ready. Get in the habit of practicing the look whenever you're out and about, in a coffee shop, at social gatherings, on the train to work. Eye contact while smiling is your main tool for communicating with people at a distance. It's the one way you can send someone a signal without having to say a word. And, by the way, most of the time it says more than words can anyway.

This kind of risk-free flirting can, and should be, a blast. There is no possibility of rejection. You can play as much as you want, try as many times as you want, and you risk absolutely nothing. People on the street will never see you again. That guy in the coffee shop will never see you again. This is a skill that you get to master without having to worry about the consequences of failing.

MATT DEMONSTRATES "THE LOOK"

In this clip I show you the look in action by demonstrating with two women live onstage.

Go to **www.gettheguybook.com/look**
Access code: **gtgbook**

Get closer

There's always the chance that the looks you send won't summon your chosen man to your side. His fear and self-doubt may be still greater than his desire. The solution? Move.

Yes, get closer.

You have made it easier for him to approach you by your eye contact and your smile. Now, make it easier by removing the need for him to have to walk across the room to you. Once you've removed the distance it becomes easy for him to casually turn his head in your direction and start a conversation, safe in the knowledge that his humiliation won't be public if the encounter goes badly.

It's easy to find reasons to get close to him. If you're in a bookstore, wander over and browse in the same section. If you're at a bar and you see him order another drink, take that opportunity to walk over and order another one yourself. If you're with a group of friends, create the chance for proximity by opening up your group and bringing new people into the conversation, so that you seem sociable and open. Use whatever excuse is handy to get close enough to him so that it will be easy for him to start a conversation.

Beyond the Smile

Maybe the party is jammed with people, loud with music and conversation, so getting closer is not an option. Or you've come with your sister-in-law who's just lost her job and the party was meant to cheer her up, so you feel you can't leave her alone if you spot a guy you're interested in. Perhaps the guy is over at the far side of the crowded room with six of his friends, one of whom looks like he might be the guy's boss. So you've made a lot of great eye contact over the course of several hours, but for whatever reason neither one of you is making a move. What do you do?

Try waving him over. Not as if you're hailing a cab, but using a subtle "come here" motion, as if you needed to tell him a secret. You've been trading looks all evening, now you're conveying that it's okay for him to wade through the crowd to get to you. Again, it's just a way of making it easy for him.

As often as not, he'll do the same gesture back to you, suggesting you be the one to come over to him. If he does, this is an opportunity to prove your value; sure, you're interested, but he's going to have to make the effort to push his way through the crowd and come to you. Stand your ground, cheekily shake your head, and wave again for him to come over, slightly more emphatically this time. It's cute, and it does the trick.

On the night I was talking to that friendly bar owner in New York, three women walked in. I made eye contact with one of them, and we must have glanced back and forth for an hour while talking to other people. I did nothing. She did nothing.

Then the dreaded scenario unfolded: her friends made their way to the door. She was leaving! As she began to walk, she looked back at me, raised her eyebrows and gave me a little wave, as if to say, "You blew it, idiot!"

I looked at her and raised my hands as if to say, "Where are you going!" She then walked over and said, "You left it too long and now I have to go!" We ended up talking long enough to exchange details, and met for a date later that week. This is proof positive that it is your gesture that will make all the difference. I didn't make the first move in this instance, and yet I coach this stuff!

Start talking

The final way of giving a guy license to speak is for you to start the conversation. "But won't making a conversation mean I'm doing all the work?" you may wonder. Well, yes . . . and no. If it's done the right way, all you are doing is attempting to get the ball rolling, which then gives him the chance to do the work of trying to be worthy of the opportunity you gave him. Just like the Victorian white handkerchief. All of this is a sort of code, but it works just the same. As for feeling as if you are doing all the work, here's the deal: I promised I would tell you what a guy is thinking. The truth is, he has as many insecurities as you do. By giving you insight into his hesitations, along with some hints for small gestures you can make to help him get over them, you can put yourself in the best possible position. And, knowing that you are taking some control helps you to feel more confident.

Ten-second rule

Most women lose amazing guys in the first ten seconds. You wouldn't believe how many of these guys are so close to starting a conversation, but bail at the last second because they lose their nerve. A friend of mine has this terrific piece of advice: "A woman should never be easy. But, in the first ten seconds of a conversation . . . be easy."

It takes balls for a guy just to approach a woman, especially in an unfamiliar social setting. The point of this rule is that you can make his approach much easier, thus much more likely. You can be a challenge later on in the conversation, but at the beginning, smile and be as approachable as possible. Give him a break for the first ten seconds of interaction. That's long enough for you to decide if he's good enough for you to bother hanging around for another ten.

The Power of the Small Favor

One of the easiest ways to draw a guy into conversation is to ask a favor. In fact, it is blindingly efficient. The line "I could really use your help with something . . ." is a magical thing to say to any guy. You might think it's not terribly clever or sophisticated, but it appeals to the part of his brain that wants to feel like a man. Something miraculous happens when he hears, "I need your help . . ." He immediately puffs out his chest, stands up straight, and thinks, Anything! The man in him is ready; even before he's heard what the favor is, he wants to do it. I said this earlier, but it bears repeating: every man wants to be around women who make him feel more like a man, and in the moment you ask us for help, you are appealing to the essential male need to be needed.

If you've ever seen an adult say to some young boys, "I need a big strong man to do this," you've seen how every boy has his hand up to volunteer; every boy wants to be strong in that moment. Men never really outgrow that childish desire to show off their strength. But here's the cool thing: asking for a favor has the same effect on a guy no matter how big or small it is. It can be something ridiculously simple, and he'll still get all those feelings of manliness.

For example, if you say, "I could really use your help with something: Can you hold my jacket for two seconds while I give these drinks to my friends?" No guy is ever going to refuse this. (If he ever does, run!) Once you've given the drinks to your friends, turn back to him, take your jacket back, and say, "Thanks so much. How's your night going?"

In this moment it doesn't even feel like you've started a conversation. It's absurdly simple, but it gives the guy the excuse he's been dying for; he can now take the lead and continue the conversation with you if he is interested. If he's not, he'll say, "You're welcome," and carry on with his night. Either way, you lose nothing. You haven't put yourself on the line because asking for a small favor is so innocuous.

Why does this work? In addition to creating a situation that instantly taps into his need to feel like a man, you're asking him specifically. By saying, "I could really use *your* help," you're personalizing your request, which makes him enjoy doing the favor because he feels selected in some way. He doesn't feel as if just anyone could have done it. You could have easily asked the man or woman standing on either side of him, and trust me, he notices the choice you made.

Benjamin Franklin once famously stated, "He that has once done you a kindness will be more ready to do you another, than he whom you yourself have obliged." This so-called Franklin Effect, put to the test in a recent study published in the journal *Human Relations*, flies in the face of what we think we know about the psychology of favors.

It's logical to assume that if someone else carries out a favor for us we feel gratitude toward them and like them better. If someone bakes you a cake, you feel more positive feelings about him or her. But the findings of the study showed that the opposite was true. When people carry out favors for us, it actually makes *them* like *us* more. In other words, the person doing us a favor feels more positive toward us because, in letting them go out of their way for our benefit, we've given them the opportunity to feel better about themselves.

The Franklin Effect works as long as the favor you ask isn't too big or demanding, and you display genuine appreciation. People enjoy the validation they receive from being able to please someone else. When this effect occurs between men and women, the result is intensified, because in asking him to help you, you've helped to make him feel like more of a man.

The Secret Ingredient
to a Memorable Conversation

When you enter a conversation with a guy you like, there's one key ingredient that assures you'll avoid sounding as if you're interviewing him for a job, questioning him for a police report, or passing the time until the party's over and you can go home.

Enter sexual tension.

From the very first words you utter, an air of sexual tension tells a guy you're different. Creating sexual tension doesn't mean you have to act sexual. At bottom, it means we are throwing in a challenge, we are adding an element of flirtation to the conversation.

Kill the small talk, say the unexpected

Once we've decided that we might be attracted to someone, slowly but surely we begin acting in ways that makes us less desirable. It's maddening!

We try harder to impress them, or lavish too much attention on them, or agree with everything they say. We start overanalyzing everything we do and lose that naturalness and sense of fun that draw people to us. Everyone seems to do this, men and women alike. With our friends we are spontaneous, relaxed, funny; we are able to make people laugh and we comfortably hold court. Then we meet someone we like and suddenly, we are boring.

Gone is our spontaneity, our willingness to tussle over opinions, our ability to tell stories in an uninhibited way that genuinely entertains. We enter the social doldrums, where we're agreeable and serious instead of playful, and engage in the dull heavy lifting of Finding Things We Have in Common.

The irony is that as we've seen, it doesn't really matter where you start a conversation. And yet, we cling to small talk because we're still somehow under the impression that this is what two people getting to know one another in a proper fashion *do*.

But small talk is deadly. The chemistry set in motion when you were across the room from each other exchanging looks is snuffed out in a minute with small talk. Now that you're standing shoulder to shoulder at your cousin's barbecue, if you resort to trading résumé-type questions, it all but guarantees all your efforts will have been in vain.

You know the questions I mean:

"So, where do you work?"

"Great, what do you do there?"

"Wow, sounds good. So where did you study?"

"Cool. What did you major in?"

The one way to guarantee that a conversation is clichéd, dull, and uninspiring is to ask questions like these.

This isn't because the people we meet are uninteresting; it's because we permit our conversations to be uninteresting. An hour trading dull, run-of-the-mill questions creates no sparks because neither party has a chance to show any personality.

Give him a test

Suppose you are standing in line at a coffee shop. You can turn to the guy behind you, and say, "Listen, I really need your help . . ." Then, after a dramatic pause, say, "I'm completely torn. I can't decide which muffin to get."

Your tone is mock serious. You're acting as if it's a serious choice by having a pretend worried look on your face, but in a way that makes it obvious that you're being playful.

The fact you've taken him by surprise will help guarantee that he'll play along. Let's suppose he suggests you try a blueberry muffin. You now have a golden opportunity to create sexual tension. If you like blueberry muffins, say, "Hmm, you have good taste. Okay, you passed."

"You've passed the test" is a genius line for flirting. It makes a guy feel as if he got something right. Even though logically he knows that the test is completely silly, emotionally his brain doesn't register that aspect. All he hears is that you are someone he has to impress, even though you communicated it through a trivial choice like whether he picked the right muffin.

What if he suggests a flavor you don't like? Suppose he suggests a lemon muffin and you can't stand them? You can still turn the moment into a flirtatious one. You can say, "Hmm . . . lemon?" then pause for a split second and say with mock despair, "Ahh, this would never work between us."

Let's examine this line more closely, because it's so powerful that we can easily miss why it works so beautifully. As soon as a man hears the line "This would never work between us," he immediately thinks, Yes, it would, and I'll prove it to you! Even though he *knows* you're only joking, once again his emotions prevent him from registering the fact. All he did was suggest a type of muffin, but he still feels like he wants to fight to impress you since he made the wrong choice. He feels like he has to get back into your good book, even though he hasn't really done anything wrong and besides, he doesn't even know you.

What has happened is that you have created a false debt. He's chosen wrong, and he wants another chance to choose right, even when he hasn't really done anything wrong. The reason this works so well is because guys like feeling as if they have to work just a little bit to get back into your good graces.

Say anything

Starting a conversation about a muffin might sound silly, but that's often the nature of flirting. Too many of us think that flirting is about being smooth and sophisticated, gazing at our newfound crush over the rim of our martini glass, when real flirting is about being spontaneous and letting go of self-consciousness.

Most of us miss out in life because we take ourselves too seriously. Flirtatious energy is youthful energy, expressed through the tiniest gestures. Stick your tongue out when you tease him, playfully bat his chest when he makes a joke. Show you possess the confidence to be spontaneous.

A conversation that crackles with possibility flows between the ridiculous and the sublime. Think about a conversation with your best friend. One minute you'll be making jokes about each other and telling funny stories, and the next you'll be having a serious conversation about your plans for your future and your passions. This is how all conversations should be: they should ebb and flow between teasing, connection, stories, jokes, and yes, even occasionally the dreaded résumé facts like where you come from and what you do for a living. However, those dull facts should only be used as conversational hooks to move between subject and topics.

It is important to understand that the way we approach our interactions says as much about who we are as what we say does. Establish a sense of playfulness and spontaneity, skip the small talk to the extent that you can, flirt and inject sexual tension into the conversation by testing him or creating a false debt. This will make for a much more successful initial conversation, and you will have more fun as well—even if he turns out to be a dud. Entertaining yourself is half the game.

Being a Leader in Your Love Life

You might be thinking that this all seems too one-sided, that this is a far cry from simply dropping your handkerchief in front of a gallant hero to signal it's time for him to do the rest.

I will say that once you incorporate some of these rituals into your day-to-day life, it won't seem like work at all. I was at a bar with my brother not long ago, and the woman standing next to me, upon receiving her glass, turned to the guy on the other side of her and said, "We're out celebrating Friday night. Cheers!" Then she clinked glasses with him. The guy was drinking some sort of fruity-looking cocktail, and she laughed and said, "Wow, I like a guy who's confident enough to order a girly drink." This exchange took less than a minute, and I could tell this young woman behaves like this wherever she goes. And she probably meets a lot of guys.

If you want to be the leader of your love life—and you do, because the alternative to sit and wait, and you've already decided against that—you must be proactive.

The Principle of Reciprocity

Being proactive doesn't mean you have to keep putting yourself out there without receiving anything in return. Rather, it's about being the one who gives to others first, then expects results.

If you compliment a guy, ask him a favor, or playfully test him and he doesn't respond, you've got your answer to the level of his interest. If you're back in the coffee shop and you ask the guy behind you what kind of muffin you should choose and he rudely responds, "I don't know. You're the one who has to eat it," you're obviously not going to continue the conversation. You've taken a moment—and it does take but a moment—to try to engage him to see if he has any interest in engaging. If he doesn't, you've invested very little of yourself, and you got to practice for the next guy.

7

From Great Conversation to First Date

You've met a terrific guy. You've traded smiles and maybe after an awkward start you're having a lively conversation in which there's some sexual tension. You're sharing jokes and anecdotes, and you've found some common ground in a place you both like to visit in Spain. He's nice enough, but you're not quite sure there's enough there to warrant seeing him again. How do you find out what he's really like? And if you do decide you like him enough to spend more time with him, how do you get him to ask to see you again? How do you move from a great chat to a date?

The Key Is Connection

Sexual tension will make him desire you physically, but connection is what makes him feel emotionally drawn to you. Many women can create sexual tension, but it's connection that makes someone truly unique. And connection starts with having better conversations. We've already learned how to at least start a conversation—and the rule there is that it doesn't matter so much what the opening to the conversation is, as long as it gets things going. Now we have to go a level deeper.

Being a great conversationalist is about two things: creating intrigue and interest, and creating emotional connection. It's not about being about to hold forth on important topics of the day, or being able to regale someone with anecdotes of all the celebrities you've met, or even being a mistress of repartee.

Many people, men and women both, err in conversation by focusing solely on themselves, rather than how they're making the other person feel. They think if they have a high-status job they'll be absolutely fascinating, and so they reel off a list of their achievements, or brag about their travels or adventures; and all the while the other person is bored to tears because she's being lectured to and has no involvement in the conversation. You know the type. The ones who never ask one question about you or your interests. You can't even call this a conversation, it's a monologue.

So how do you make the most out of a connection and actually get to know someone?

Seek values, not facts

What we really want to know about someone in our first conversations is what kind of person he or she is. You want to know if he shares your values, whether he's ambitious, kind, intellectual, and curious. You aren't going to find out these things by knowing that he works in investment banking, lives downtown, and likes to go to the movies.

Suppose you're stuck on talking about work and he says, "I hate my job, it's really boring." A good conversationalist has developed the ability to move the topic into more intriguing territory. He hates his job? You can then ask, "If every career in the world paid the same money, what would you be doing? Or, "If money wasn't an issue, what would you be doing tomorrow?" Or, "Would you rather earn a hundred thousand dollars a year doing a job you hate, or forty thousand a year doing a job you love?"

Now you're inviting him to discuss his passions and what he finds meaningful in life. You've transformed his negative remark about hating his job into a chance for him to open up about the things he really cares about. Now you're going to find out what he really values most. Then you can just follow up with a why question; now you're in a position to find out a lot about him pretty quickly.

If he chooses the $100K job, ask him why. It might be because he values security and likes to play it safe. It might be because he is adventurous and would love to have the money to travel. Or it might be just because he likes to live a luxury lifestyle. None of these are bad reasons, they just express different values. That's why it's crucial that you follow up with the obvious question: "Why that choice?" If he goes for the money, what would he spend it on? If he goes for the $40K dream job, what is that job? And what's so special about it that he wouldn't care about having as much money? So no matter what he answers, you are going to get a very clear glimpse of what he strives for in life.

Moving the conversation from the logical to the emotional creates connection. Logical questions are simply placeholders in an interaction. Emotion-based questions reveal a guy's true values.

By asking questions that lead a guy to talk about his interests or passions, you've accomplished two things. You open up the conversation so he can ask similar questions of you and in turn get to know you as well. It also creates a chance for him to experience a rush of positive feelings, which he'll then associate with talking to you. Connection occurs because he begins to see you as someone who brings out different parts of him. He feels as if he's shared something personal with you that he probably doesn't even share with his friends.

And by the way, if these questions feel like they are coming out of the blue, just say, "A friend asked me an interesting question the other day." Your "friend," whether she exists or not, is one of your best wingwomen when it comes to making conversations.

How to see if he shares your values

During the first conversation you have with a guy, your primary task is see if you have any chemistry. Is there that spark that encourages you to get to know him better? Do you want to reveal more of yourself to him? The presence of this spark requires more than someone who pushes your buttons sexually; you also find him exciting upon discovering he shares your values.

Let's say one of your requirements for a boyfriend is that he share your love of adventure. Maybe you love to travel and visit exotic locations, or maybe you're a thrill seeker and want to visit strange and even dangerous places. In that case, you're going to need someone adventurous.

During that first conversation, dive in. Ask, "If you could wake up anywhere in the world tomorrow, where would it be?" Or, "If you could drop everything and hop on a plane, where would you go?"

Most women would wait until the first date (or even second or third) to discover whether the guy shared her love of travel and adventure. But why wait? If we are not using conversation to dig and see if there's connection, we are wasting our time.

Other Ways to Make the Conversation Great

So now that you are a good conversationalist, there's one pretty big problem: any constructive conversation requires two people, and chances are good that the guy is still stuck in the small-talk rut.

There is one surefire principle that every good conversationalist knows: *obvious questions don't require obvious answers.*

What have you been up to? Where are you from? What do you do for a living? Just because a lot of the guys you meet resort to these conversation-killing questions doesn't mean you have to give the obvious answers.

Let's say a guy asks how your day was, you could either respond the way everyone else does, "Good, thanks." Or you can turn the question on its ear and in doing so send the conversation into a more interesting direction.

Build intrigue:

"I feel great," you might say. "I solved a big problem today so I'm in a good mood." (He's going to want to know what the problem you solved was.)

Pose a more interesting question:

"I've been consumed with a question my friend asked me. Would you rather your partner sleep with someone else, or fall in love with someone else? What do you think?" (Wow, what does he think?)

Get mock-serious:

"I feel amazing. I've got this new iPhone and it's completely changed my whole life. I'm 50 percent more trendy. But I need more apps so I can look cool. What's the best one to download?"

Tease him:

"I'm awesome. I've just been telling my friend how this new shampoo has made my hair softer than ever. Everyone keeps asking me what my secret is." Then if he tries to feel your hair, withdraw quickly and jokingly say, "No! You're not allowed to touch it." Alternatively, let him touch it and say, "That'll be ten dollars."

We can't control what other people say, but we can always control our responses to them. You can turn the most overused question of all time (What have you been up to?) into any kind of conversation you'd like to have. You don't even have to mention your day at all. You could just say, "I've been really excited for the last two weeks—I'm going to Africa next month," which allows you to talk about something that both excites you and conveys that you're a woman with an interesting life. The boring stuff that goes on in our regular day just doesn't matter.

People only ever ask each other, "How was your day?" because they can't think of anything else to say. Apart from our mothers and our best friends, no one gives the slightest crap what happened in our day, especially when they meet us for the first time.

Get the Date

I'm not a fan of the formal date. The traditional dinner-and-a-movie is rigid and uninspired, not to mention agonizing. The two of you are forced to sit across from each other and eat without spilling anything on yourselves or letting the conversation flag.

We need a looser interpretation of the word "date." I suggest we all start thinking of it as a meet-up instead. A meet-up can be as casual or as formal as we want. Unlike a date, a meet-up doesn't have to last an entire evening. A good meet-up can be as short as thirty minutes.

You could have a meet-up for Sunday brunch, or just trying the ice cream in that cute place that's opened near where you work. It could be bringing him along to something you're doing with friends: "I'm going to this picnic/music gig/comedy event/zoo. You should come!"

When we think of dating in more informal terms, it removes the pressure of arranging a date. If you're now creating sexual tension, chemistry, and connection in your conversations, the transition to a date will become a natural part of the connection.

Suppose you're at a get-together chatting with a guy and it's going great, and your friend comes up and says, "We're leaving now. Come on, let's go." You want to make sure you get this guy's phone number before you are dragged off and lose the opportunity, but now you're in the awkward position of having to ask for his number straight out. So what can you do to make it easier?

Sowing the seeds of a meet-up

Generally, you know pretty quickly during an exchange with a guy whether you'd like to spend more time with him. There's always the chance that something might happen further along in the conversation to turn you off, but the best way to clear the way for the date is to plant the idea early in the interaction. This makes the eventual exchange of numbers easier because now you have a reason to ask for his information.

You're not actually asking for a date, you're just floating the idea of a meet-up, usually in a half-serious, playful manner.

> You: "All the guys I know keep telling me to see *[insert title of popular guy movie here]* but I haven't seen it yet. Is it really that good?" (Bonus points here for displaying your interest in a movie that appeals to him.)
> THE GUY: "No, I haven't, but I want to."

You: "We might be the only people left on planet earth who haven't seen it yet! We should go!"

THE GUY: "Sounds like an idea."

You: "But wait, are you a popcorn- or ice-cream-at-the-movies sort of person?" (Giving him a test.)

THE GUY: "Gotta have popcorn at the movies. With butter."

You: "Okay, you can come! If you said ice cream I'd have to uninvite you." (He passed!)

Then, just leave it at that. You haven't made specific plans, but you've seeded the idea of going on a date, and also created more excitement and connection by testing him.

Even though you're being playful, what it communicates to the guy is that while you've suggested meeting up, he hasn't got you yet. It's irrational, but his brain still registers that he has had that test to pass. This way, you're the one bringing up the idea of meeting up, yet it's still going to be a challenge for him.

One step forward, one step back

This next bit of advice is going to feel a little difficult to pull off. You'll suddenly get nervous and think, This guy seems great—I don't want to scare him off. This is what most of us do when we feel attracted to someone. We want to be accommodating and nice, and clear every obstacle along the way to a potential relationship. We feel that if we're challenging in any way, we might blow it. But it's precisely these little challenges that convey to a guy that you're a high-value woman worth pursuing. He's going to find you intriguing because you have standards. This is where we pull all of the pieces together.

I want to step back for a moment. When I first started my business I would rush to take any gig. I made myself available at all times. Slowly, my schedule started to become full, and I simply couldn't accept every job that came my way, or I would have to make the new client wait until I could fit them into my schedule. Without understanding what I was doing, I was creating value for my time and services. Once I stopped saying yes to everything, my value increased and demand for my time grew. Not being too available actually increased demand and respect for my time.

In relationships, simply not being available at every moment places value on your time. Let him know that you are available, but not at any moment. You may like this guy a lot, but don't go out of your way to be available to him. I am not talking about playing hard-to-get or playing mind games. Since you have high standards, you want to make sure that he understands that although you are giving him your number you aren't going to automatically be available to him whenever he calls.

Anytime you take the initiative with a guy, it's also effective to pull back a bit. You're being slightly forward, then inviting him to do more. You are letting him have your number, but you are also telling him that you're high value and that it's still possible that he could blow it. You can say something playfully arrogant like "Okay, here's my number, but no calling me day and night telling me you miss me." Alternatively, you can say, "If we get along over the phone we can hang out sometime." This shows he's got more convincing to do over the phone and makes him feel he has to earn the right to spend time with you.

———

Seeding the idea of a date makes the moment of actual number swapping less harrowing. You've already established something you both want to do. When it comes time to part, you can easily say something like "Hey, I've got to go. Let me give you my number and we'll hit that film festival some time." Or, "I have to get back to my friends. I shouldn't even be talking to you, we're supposed to be having a girls' night out, but take my number and maybe we can do something sometime."

Notice, the word "date" is never mentioned. You're just meeting up. However, during the conversation you'll have built up enough chemistry and sexual tension so he'll understand that it's not just going to be two buddies hanging out. Now the ball is in his court, but it makes it so simple for him. You already have the first date arranged.

What you're conveying is: *I'm a busy person, but you seem fun, so let me grab your number and when we get time we'll do something.* If he's the one who's taking off, then my advice would be to wait for him to ask for your number. But if you sense he's being too shy, give him your number and say to him, "Text me your number and I'll let you know when I'm going to that film festival."

Your tone here is casual and matter-of-fact. It works because you say it as though you were going to the festival whether he's interested or not. This is also a great frame of mind to have when you arrange a date. He is welcome to join you in your fabulous life, but you're going on with or without him.

8

The Joy of Text

Once you've traded numbers, let the texting begin!

While I'm loose about what defines a date, I'm pretty strict about texting. It's one of those things that, just because we can do it, that doesn't mean we should do it. Or rather, we should take care to do it with restraint.

Whether you've just met or have been dating for months, texts should only ever be used for two things: entertainment and logistics.

Logistics are pretty self-explanatory. You're running late; the café where you were going to meet is closed on Sunday; the president's in town and the street is cordoned off; the house is on fire and you have to reschedule—these are excellent reasons to pop out a text.

The other reason you should text is to create intrigue, interest, and value. Your texts should be cheeky, flirty, and fun. They should display your wit and humor, or even just *bait* the guy.

For example, you can message a guy saying, "I was watching a film and just realized, you really remind me of Bruce Willis . . . xo." But don't tell him why. When he asks why—and he will—toss out a little detail they share, like they raise their eyebrow the same way, or have an intense stare, or they both look like the kind of guy who would wear a vest, or they are both cool under pressure.

Your aim is to be either slightly complimentary or ambiguous. If it's complimentary, don't make it overly complimentary (e.g., "because you're both so sexy"). But don't make it insulting either. The best way is to make it a tongue-in-cheek compliment.

Or, send a teasing text, which is the equivalent of giving a guy a shoulder nudge. It's enough to get his attention, but in a way that makes him want to push back a little. After a date, you might text something like this: "I just thought you should know, I saw a lot of Whitney Houston on your iPod last night. Should I be concerned? . . . xo." Or play it the other way, and mention something that you like: "I've never seen a man with so much '80s music on his iPod. Seriously impressed . . . xo." This one works great because he feels like he's passed a test he didn't know he was taking.

Texts are squibs of communication meant to spike his interest, not vehicles for endless small talk or a substitute for genuine conversation. The trick with texting is to be sparing but effective. There's no room for long essays and catching up on everything that's going on. Save that conversation for when you see him in person.

Texting a guy back and forth for hours might make you feel like you're building rapport, but this is deceptive. If you get too intimate and confessional over texting (no drunk texting!), the next time you meet up again your interaction may feel awkward because now you'll have a connection and intimacy in your text relationship that you don't possess in real life.

The Text You Never Want to Send

In the same way our conversations can boring, so can people's autopilot text conversation. One of the worst texts to send anyone is "I'm so bored. What u been up to? xo."

This text is a downer. It says to a guy that you're bored, and therefore in need of entertainment. It also gives him no opportunity to be playful, to flirt, to tease, or to say something cheeky.

When a guy receives a text from you, he should feel a little spike of emotion. Now, that emotion might just be amusement at something funny you said, or it might be intrigue, or he might smile because it was a little flirtatious, anything other than going through routine stuff like having to write about his day on a text message. If you're stumped, just ask for an opinion. Say "My friends are I are going to watch a horror film tonight, but I never watch scary films. Any recommendations?"

The Text That Gets Him to Ask You Out

What if you met a guy and had a terrific conversation, you've exchanged numbers, but a few days have passed and you haven't heard from him?

The reason could be that he's lost interest, but never assume. It might be that he's genuinely in the weeds at work and can't think about his love life this week.

But if the trail seems to have gone cold, you could write the guy off and put your interaction behind you, but there is a text you can send that will allow you to be certain.

Send this text around 9 p.m. Why so specific? Because you already need to be out for the night, at a party, pub, concert, art opening, bowling tournament. You want to send it when it's a little bit too late for him to actually come and meet up with you; the whole point is that the hour is unreasonable. And then you send him this: "I'm down at the Jazz Bar. The music's amazing, you should come!"

You tell him where you are and why it's great, and end by saying, "You should come."

"You should come!" is a hugely confident line. It shows your level of certainty. The point of the clarifier text is to give him a chance to do something. It puts the ball entirely in his court. You are telling him that you are already out and having a good time with people, so the text doesn't sound desperate. But you are also telling him that it would be cool if he were there with you.

But, here's the thing: You don't actually expect him to show up. That's why you ask it when it's quite late, as though it's an afterthought. Why? Because then, if he can't come but he still wants to see you, he'll text you back offering a countersuggestion to meet up another time. Or, if by chance he does decide to come, you are already out and he can just join you. You win either way. And if he isn't interested at all, then you don't lose anything anyway. You're in the same position as before, and you haven't put yourself on the line by asking him out on a date.

Only send this text when you are actually out somewhere. Don't be sitting in the bathtub expecting him not to show up! If he likes you, there is a chance he might come.

Make a Statement

Often when texting it's much more powerful to use a statement than a question. If you text a guy saying, "We're all going to that new restaurant in town later tonight. Come to dinner!" it communicates a level of confidence and certainty that guys aren't used to hearing from a woman. It's a way of saying, "I'm going to this cool place with cool people, and you should come join us." If he likes you, all he has to do is say yes. And if he can't make it that night, he'll just reschedule for another time, in which case you've got him arranging the date. It's perfect because it makes things so elegant.

When you use a confident statement like "You should come join us," it takes choice out of the equation. It removes the entire ordeal of debating about when and where you're going to meet, and trying to see how your schedules fit for the next week. If I ask, "Do you want to go on a date next week?" there are suddenly a lot of variables that need to be addressed: Do you want to? If you do, are you available? If so, when are you available? What do you want to do? Where do you want to go? It starts to seem like a lot of work. But when you tell a guy where you are, what you're doing, and that he should just come, he can focus on the fun he's going to have when he meets up with you.

AVOID THIS TEXT MESSAGE AT ALL COSTS

While we are on the subject of text messages, in this clip I discuss both the ideal text to send to a guy you like and an awful text that will kill attraction faster than socks in sandals.

Go to **www.gettheguybook.com/text**
Access code: **gtgbook**

9

A Word About Online Dating

I am often asked questions about online dating. While I am a proponent of the flesh-and-blood connection first and foremost, I can't deny the popularity and allure—for some—of the cyberconnection. And while I admit that it is not impossible to find the love of your life online, it does tend to be more difficult.

As you recall from the first chapter of the book, the philosophy of the funnel applies here. I like to think about the Internet as a way of contributing to the first funnel of men you will meet.

Time is our most valuable resource, and when you find guys online you go on a lot more first dates. In fact, you risk creating a love life that consists of *only* first dates. The reason, of course, is that online dating sites are really only a way to find a list of people interested in dating, accompanied by a few squibs of information that, while interesting, might not really matter in the long run.

The confidence, charisma, and je ne sais quoi that draw us to one person and not another are virtually impossible to demonstrate in a dating profile, even by someone who expresses himself well. The result is that even though you may learn from his profile that he likes kung fu movies, extreme Frisbee, and opera, you still have to meet him to discern whether there's even a remote possibility of attraction.

The most revolutionary idea in this book is that there are powerful tools for creating attraction and connection no matter what you look like, what you do for a living, or how old you are. Online dating, with its focus on exactly these things, obliterates your chances to use these tools.

Have you ever been attracted to someone who wasn't your type? Have you ever been uninterested in someone until you sat with them and had a conversation for half an hour, only to realize you were completely captivated by them? Of course you have.

That's because genuine attraction is a complicated spectrum of the way we move, walk, talk, and gesture; the beliefs we hold and the conviction with which we communicate them; the way our muscles move in our face when we smile; the subtle differences between a look of shyness and a look of playfulness; our reactions to situations and the way we deal with life. All of which cannot possibly be communicated through a profile.

But online dating is here to stay. Now a billion-dollar industry, and the third most popular way people meet (through work and school is most common, followed by an introduction made by a friend or family member), it can be a useful tool, as long as it doesn't become a crutch. It gives you immediate access to guys no matter where you are, offers a pool of guys who are, ostensibly, single and seeking the same thing you're seeking, and provides enough information to know whether a guy is a complete write-off. Also, if you do decide to meet one, it affords you something to talk about.

Before You Log On

In order to make the most of what online dating has to offer, it helps to approach it with a mindset that will help you accomplish your goals. You don't want to fall into the trap of spending hours alone online when you could be out in the real world meeting flesh-and-blood men. So, before you put on your fuzzy slippers, grab that cup of hot cocoa, and curl up with your laptop, here are some important things to remember.

Beware the false sense of ease

Online dating makes meeting someone new seductively easy. We see someone we like and we can message them instantly, without having to take the personal risk inherent in initiating a face-to-face interaction. All well and good, unless—as is so often the case—e-mailing, texting, and IMing become a substitute for actually going out and meeting people. Never forget that the end goal is to go on real dates, not sit at home in our pajamas communicating via the Internet. The fantasy of what someone *might* be like when we talk to them online is meaningless unless we actually progress to the point of meeting them.

It solves only one part of the process

To think that the only problem in your love life is that you're just not meeting people is a fallacy. It's part of the problem, certainly, but having gathered two dozen profiles of possible guys you'd like to date has nothing to do with the other aspects of finding and getting the guy. Online dating should be used only to set up real dates, to get you face-to-face with Mr. Maybe so you can further practice and hone your other skills.

Resist becoming overly fussy

People tend to get very fussy very quickly when poring over online profiles, the fallout from having so many strangers to choose from. The typical end result is that we look for someone to match every single one of our criteria. We stop giving people a chance. At the beginning of this book we talked about the power of throwing the net wide and meeting a lot of men. While reading through profiles might seem like you're "meeting" a lot of men, all most people do is eliminate people based on the flimsiest of pretenses.

Making it your only method

It's not uncommon for people to feel that if by signing up, they're being proactive in their love lives. The next step is that they stop going out completely and sit around in their apartment scrolling through profiles. Use online dating as an adjunct; it works best when combined with all of the other methods demonstrated in this book. You never know when you are going to run into someone you are attracted to in real life. Don't let being online make you miss those chances.

Rejection

Make no mistake about it, people are rejected online, just as they are in real life. When it happens, remember that this is completely normal. Not everyone is supposed to want you or even like you. When I first started making videos on YouTube, I would ignore the positive comments and focus solely on the negative ones. It affected me until I realized that it was impossible to avoid. At least 10 percent of people will dislike us no matter what we do. And that will always be the case. It's okay.

Assuming you're the only one

When a guy first signs up on an online dating site, there's a high probability that he's talking to a lot of women at the same time. If he is, this is unlikely to change until you in meet in person and decide to move forward. The extent to which guys are leading on multiple women varies between sites, and it's more likely to happen on free sites, but it *will* happen, probably to everyone. Don't take it personally; just establish the boundaries once it gets more serious.

Writing the All-Important Profile

Unlike real-life interactions, where moment to moment you're giving and receiving many clues about a guy you've just met, when you're trying to connect with someone online everything rests on the quality of your profile. (No pressure there!) Below are a few tips for increasing the odds that someone you might want to date finds you.

Don't try to reinvent the wheel

Once you've read twenty different profiles you'll begin to see a pattern. No profile is so unique that it hasn't been done before; if you do come across one that's written in the form of a Shakespearian sonnet, you can be pretty confident that the guy is trying too hard. Avoid trying to be too funny, too serious, or too quirky. Just think about what you really want to convey about yourself and figure out a simple way to say it.

Keep it brief

As much as most of us love talking about ourselves and our opinions, nobody cares that much about someone who's just popped up on their screen. It's fascinating to watch someone when they first join an online dating site. The first profile they come upon is read with love and care. They read every word and consider the things that are said. The next profile is given slightly less time. Once the person realizes just how many profiles there are, they start skimming them, and before they know it, they are treating them like advertisements in a cheap magazine, barely allowing their eyes to acknowledge the page in front of them.

Great advertisers learn that a good headline and punchy ideas are better than too much explanatory text. When people first see your profile, they're not buying into the detail, they're buying into the idea of you. In fact, the more detail you give someone, the more reasons you give them to say no. This is especially the case with men, most of whom are skimmers at best.

This doesn't mean you should give so little information that they know nothing about you. Aim to strike a balance: provide enough information to give them a good sense of you but keep it short enough so they don't get distracted by the fifteen other things popping up on Skype, Facebook, Twitter, and their TV at the same time.

Remember, once a guy has a sense of who you are, he'll fill in the blanks himself. If the first 5 percent of you seems attractive, he will use it to create an attractive image of the other 95 percent he doesn't know.

Don't resort to long lists

"I'm friendly, open, outgoing, fun, and adventurous . . ."

Who cares? Not me, not you, not anyone else. Why? Because talk is cheap. It's better to convey who you are either through your actions, your stories, or by talking about what you love and hate than by writing a long list of adjectives. The old adage remains true here: show, don't tell. Now, it's hard to show until you meet someone in person, but you can do a much better job of selling your best qualities with the right language. "One of the most important people in the world to me is my little sister. I'd do anything for her" (showing) is much more compelling than "I'm a really loving person" (telling).

"Why" tells him more than "what"

Just as in conversation, it's more important in your profile to say why you love something than to tell what it is. If you talk about a movie you like, say why you like it. People may not relate to the movie, but they may relate to your reasons. It's the same with your profession.

Someone may not relate to your job, but they may relate to why you like your job.

Rather than spouting facts about yourself, show who you are through your stories and your opinions.

Don't be preachy

In an effort to show enthusiasm, some profile writers lapse into rants. They rail against guys who play games, or how everyone should be a vegan, and in doing so come off as judgmental and inflexible. The best profiles describe in a passionate (and often playful) manner the writer's likes and dislikes about life. Having a sense of humor about yourself, and your opinions, is key.

Also try to avoid including deal breakers. "Not interested in anyone who drives a minivan." You may think you're being candid about what you don't want, but he's only looking at your profile, not marrying you. Keep an open mind.

Don't be the Everything Girl

I'm outdoorsy, but I love dressing up. I'm really girly, but I watch tons of football. I love trashy novels, but I'm also crazy about books on neuroscience. I love all types of music. By trying to appeal to all men, you appeal to no one. Choose your audience and be honest about your likes and dislikes. You cannot relate to everyone.

Do brag about yourself, but indirectly

A great way to brag about yourself without being too direct about it is to talk about how your friends would describe you: "My friends would say I don't have any trouble getting attention from guys, but the truth is it's rare that I meet the type of guy I really want to be with." This way you're able to demonstrate a positive attribute—in this case that you are in demand—but you're able to distance yourself from it. Notice this particular line is followed up with talking about how you find it difficult to meet someone who meets your standards for what you want in a relationship.

Do include the type of guy you're looking for

People often forget that as much as their profile is there to sell themselves, it's also a great tool for preframing how you want the guy to act around you. An example of preframing would be to say things like "I'm looking for someone who isn't cynical and appreciates the little things in life" or "I need a guy who loves to read and talk about books as much as I do." This does several things.

First, it tells anyone reading your profile that you don't let just anyone into your life. This raises your value and creates an element of challenge for him. Second, it gives him a clear indicator of how he needs to act around you in order to get you attracted. If he hasn't read a book since high school, you can bet he's going to remedy that before you get together. It's effectively a way of dictating his behavior before he's even met you.

Sending Messages That Matter

To reiterate, the best way to use an online dating site is to treat it merely as a directory. Your aim should always be to meet in person, not to talk online. Getting to your first meeting with a guy whose profile you like should always be your goal. You may already feel there's a connection because you appear to have things in common, but it's important to confirm this in some small way through your messages. Not to mention that if you try to arrange a meeting with the first message you send, your perceived value will likely go down in his eyes.

Your first message (assuming you are making the first move) can simply be a comment about something you have seen on his profile—reference a quote he likes, his favorite movie, or something funny or light that annoys both of you.

The major advantage of meeting people online over meeting people in person is that you already know enough about them to say something that relates directly to them: "I saw that one of your favorite movies is *Titanic*, and I wanted to commend you on being the only guy here who's man enough to admit it!" What guy could resist sending you a reply?

This type of message builds far more intrigue than simply saying, "Hey, how you doing?" Also, make it a point to avoid questions that elicit yes or no responses, which stops the flow of communication dead in its tracks.

Get on the Phone ASAP

After you've established a connection, it's important to move things offline as soon as you can. Messaging online is the least personal way of communicating. Continuing to associate online leaves both parties in a sort of holding pattern; both of you could be, and probably are, messaging many people. Exchanging phone numbers, on the other hand, is more intimate and will build connection more quickly.

Once you feel ready, if he hasn't already, suggest he text you instead because you've had enough of messaging through the site. This has the added bonus of showing that you're not an online dating addict and have no desire to remain attached to the site.

When the moment is right, have him call you for a brief chat. You can always say in a text, "Give me a call sometime and we'll see if we really get on or if we hate each other!" This playfully sets up a challenge for him, as it shows you are not ready to meet in person until you've really established that he's worth it. Phone calls will save you a lot of time by weeding out people with whom you have no real connection.

Arranging to Meet

I've heard stories of people spending over a year e-mailing and messaging each other, only to find out there's no chemistry between them when they finally lay eyes on each other. Again, this is why it's important to arrange to meet a guy you like face-to-face as soon as possible. Normally when we meet someone we're into, we arrange a date with them *because* there's chemistry. With online dating, we arrange it to *find out* if there's chemistry.

THE GOOD, THE BAD, AND THE BORING

Online dating can be overwhelming when you first start and soul destroying after many fruitless hours of trying. Either way, I have something for you that will help drastically change the results you get from online dating.

Go to **www.gettheguybook.com/onlinedating**
Access code: **gtgbook**

PART TWO

Get the Guy

10

≡

The Ultimate Formula for Attraction

There's a difference between riding a giddy, short-lived high when you meet a cute guy and creating the enduring attraction that leads to a long-term relationship. Now that you have done the work to find the guy, I want to guide you through the process of transforming that first moment of enchantment into deep and perhaps lasting attachment. This interim period is rarely discussed; people are quick to tell you how to get dates and quick to tell you when to give him an ultimatum about commitment, but few can tell you how to navigate the tricky time in between.

Genuine, deep, and long-lasting attraction starts to grow from the moment a guy falls asleep thinking about the amazing woman he's just met. He experiences a range of feelings: he can't wait until the next time he sees her, replaying the events of the evening and wondering if she will really want to see him again. Yes, guys do that too. Being able to create such a feeling is the key to creating attraction. It's more than connection or friendship or just sexual interest.

The ability to be sexy, charismatic, and sought after is the result of how we behave. Attractiveness to the opposite sex is not some mystical energy bestowed upon a chosen few. Even if it is seems to come easier to some and not to others, the qualities and behaviors that create attraction can be learned and reproduced. As Oscar Wilde once said, "Success is a science; if you have the conditions you get the result."

Why Do We Need a Formula? Isn't Attraction Just Natural?

Do you know any naturally positive people who, when asked about their sunny outlook, can't really explain it? But, when you observe their habits, how they deal with problems, how they choose to frame the events of their lives, and the way they live, you can see quite clearly some clues to their optimism. They aren't "naturally" anything; they create the conditions.

So it is with attraction. Just because attraction seems to happen naturally, that doesn't mean it's random. I've spent years working to understand attraction. I've studied and absorbed every theory I can find. The result is a formula that, if followed, creates the conditions for developing lasting attraction.

This doesn't mean that you can't be who you are. Everyone, men and women alike, has different qualities they look for in people, certain values they seek out, and physical types to which they respond. However, the principles of what makes a woman attractive to a man remain the same. There are patterns of behavior that all attractive women exhibit.

The formula for attraction provides guiding principles only. It's not a rigorous code meant to suck all spontaneity and excitement out of your love life. I am a complete romantic, so for me the absolute joy of life is found in those spontaneous moments where attraction unexpectedly takes root. Some of my most cherished relationships have come out of those completely unexpected moments.

One day a friend and I were walking down the street and we passed two women. I traded a look with one of them and was immediately attracted to her, but I just kept on walking. After about fifteen seconds my friend said, "If you don't go back and speak to her, I'm going to tell all of your clients you don't practice what you preach." This was a fairly busy London street, and by now she was at the other end of the block. I turned and ran to catch up with her. I was panting and out of breath when I reached them, not my smoothest moment. I asked them where they were from—a pretty lame line, but saying something is always better than saying nothing.

My girl's friend looked me up and down and tried to pull her away, but then my girl said something to her friend in Spanish and smiled at me. I had no idea what she'd said, but she and her friend agreed to go for a drink with us. We spent the next eighteen months in an incredibly passionate relationship, during which I found out what she'd said to her friend that day: "He's wearing cufflinks. What's the worst that can happen?"

Amazing things can happen during tiny, unexpected moments, but that doesn't mean we should approach our love lives in a haphazard manner.

But most of us approach our love lives in a completely haphazard manner. We stumble around, come on too strong or not strong enough, are overcome by shyness or chattiness, or drink too much and go on a bad-joke-telling spree. We don't have a clue what we're doing, aside from waiting for a miracle.

The Formula

I'm always looking to create strategies that people can replicate. By studying over a hundred thousand women and how they interact with men, I've been able to see what patterns they consistently show. What follows may seem a little prescribed, but I can tell you firsthand that every time a high-value guy has been attracted to you, you were following this formula, whether you were aware of it or not.

Visual Chemistry + Perceived Challenge + Perceived Value + Connection = Deep and Lasting Attraction

Let's break down each of the attributes of the formula.

Visual chemistry

Where does physical desire come from? What causes someone to want you?

The obvious answer, and the one responsible for most myths surrounding romance, is your looks. I'm going to put it to rest right here, right now. You don't have to be drop-dead gorgeous to find attraction. You don't have to have a perfect figure, porcelain skin, and the smile of a model in a toothpaste ad.

Of course looks matter. I'm not going to lie to you about how men really are; part of my mission is to help you understand male psychology. It would be disingenuous of me to say that looks don't feature at all on a man's radar, or that a man doesn't have an image in his mind of the perfect woman. If you ask any guy what his ideal woman looks like, he'll reel off a list of objectively beautiful traits. He'll say he only goes for brunettes. Or he's a leg man. Or he needs a woman with blue eyes, or huge breasts. These are simply conditioned responses based on what he sees in magazines, TV, and movies. In reality, these specifically called-out characteristics have no real bearing on what makes him melt. They may be what he fantasizes about, but they're not what are ultimately going to attract him for the long run.

You certainly don't need to look like a supermodel in order to attract amazing guys. If only raving beauties were capable of attracting men, there would never be any single actresses or models, and every woman who was merely cute, pretty, or charming would die an old maid. You would also never see any below-average-looking married people. (Have you ever walked past someone you think is homely holding his or her mate's hand and thought, Even *they've* found someone?) There is someone for everyone.

Just being beautiful is not going to keep a guy around. As Michael Caine said in the movie *Alfie*, "Whenever you meet a beautiful woman, just remember somewhere there's a man who's sick of shagging her." Beautiful movie stars are unhappy in love all the time, and many a saucy girl-next-door type is beating away the guys with a stick. Why is this?

Because there's a huge difference between *objective* beauty and *perceived* beauty.

Objective beauty is not constant and changes over time. Looks go in and out of fashion, decade by decade. In the twenty-first century, one might say that toned abs, tanned skin, and straight hair are considered beautiful, whereas in the Renaissance, softer and larger women with pale skin and masses of thick, wavy hair were the ones who made men swoon. Even the universally acclaimed beauties of the 1950s possessed different body types than those we value today. Marilyn Monroe, still considered one of the most stunning, sexy women in history, had short, wavy hair, and might be considered chubby and out-of-shape by today's standards.

Perceived beauty, which creates visual chemistry, on the other hand, occurs when one becomes attractive through behavior. How charismatic you are in conversation, how you carry yourself, your ability to exude both confidence and playful energy, and how comfortable you are in creating sexual tension—these behaviors are what creates the perception of beauty.

None of these qualities have anything to do with how objectively beautiful you may or may not be. No one can influence the cultural standards of objective beauty, but we all have massive influence over our own perceived beauty. Luckily for us, when it comes to attraction and relationships, perceived beauty is the only kind that matters.

This explains why we can become extremely attracted to someone who on paper isn't our type. It's also why men will often be attracted initially to a woman based on her looks, and then after a tedious ten-minute conversation find her completely unsexy, and even become turned off by how boring or superficial they find her. Such a turnoff can even happen within seconds of hearing her speak. Of course, the opposite also happens more than you think. A guy meets a woman he initially has no attraction to, and then she says or does something that captures his attention in a new way and BAM!—it's like a thunderbolt hit him.

Possessing objective beauty is sometimes useful for gaining initial attention, but if the spark a man feels is to grow into a flame, much more has to be going on. Indeed, the objectively beautiful woman often finds getting and keeping a guy much harder than does the woman of perceived beauty. When a great-looking woman is used to getting attention only for her looks, she may come to rely on that aspect of herself, leaving little incentive to work on the parts of her personality that bring long-term attraction. Her character remains underdeveloped because she's never had to rely on it to gain attention. I've often heard men complain about meeting an objectively beautiful woman with a disappointing personality. It's like seeing a bright shiny Ferrari, only to find that it contains a V-4 engine. No matter how slick the body of the car is, without quality components, it's of no real value.

When this happens, beauty becomes a liability.

Again, I'm not saying that looks are meaningless. Gorgeous women will always receive a lot of attention. But attention alone can fizzle out after a week, a month, a year, or even a single night. It is no guarantee of lasting attraction. You can't build a successful long-term relationship on initial attention.

Before I started hosting my Get the Guy weekend seminars, I primarily coached men. At the beginning of the seminar I would ask them to describe the woman of their dreams. I was always surprised that rather than a superficial list of physical traits, a majority produced an exhaustive list of character traits. They longed for a partner who was confident, sexy, playful, independent, nurturing, sweet, caring, warm, feisty. When I pressed them further and asked, "What would she look like?" they would offer up the usual assortment of blondes, brunettes, and redheads. What is interesting about this is that the first response was never about looks, and when I pressed them to offer physical attributes, their responses were never expressed with as much passion as the first set of traits.

So, just because a guy says, "I'm into blondes," it doesn't mean anything. I have a friend who claimed to be into blondes. Out of six girlfriends, five were brunettes. Why? Because what he superficially thinks he wants and what actually creates real attraction are two entirely different things. Attraction is emotional, not logical. Attraction is created by hundreds of small behaviors and actions over time, behaviors that can be learned, practiced, and put in the service of creating chemistry with a guy you like. Trust me, if you take this on and believe it, your guy will find you beautiful for all the right reasons, reasons that are specific to you and only you. You've heard this a million times, but it bears repeating here: visual chemistry comes from inner beauty. And any man in love will find his beloved beautiful.

Perceived challenge

We all appreciate the things we have to work for and place less value on things we're given for free. The people we find ourselves attracted to are those whose attention we've had to earn. A woman with high standards is effortlessly attractive to men, because she gives them something to which they must aspire.

A high-value woman will always appear to be a challenge, because the guy she just met doesn't know her standards and will always
be testing them.

Look at the familiar scenario of a guy taking a woman home at
the end of the night. He is a guy, and because he's a guy, he's going
to see about the possibility of having sex. If she's a high-value woman,
and one of her standards is no sex on the first date, she's going to make
it clear that it's not going to happen. This doesn't mean she's going to
get all high and mighty and mood-killing. Instead she might say, "As
cute as you are, I couldn't do that, because I am a lady." She's tongue-
in-cheek, but she also means it.

Even though he's getting turned down, the guy remains attracted,
because she's not only displaying her integrity, she's doing so in a way
that's playful and flattering. She's not saying never, she's just saying
not now. She's adhering to her standards, even though she finds him
attractive.

This isn't to say that being a perceived challenge is only about
will-she-or-won't-she have sex, although this is a common arena
in which being a perceived challenge is played out. Some women
have guys chasing them in the initial stages of their courtship by
presenting themselves as someone who has to be earned. Where
they crr is in making their sexuality their only power. The predict-
able result is that the guy chases her for as long as she withholds
sex. Once he has her, the challenge is over. The attraction was all
in the chase.

A woman can fail to be perceived as a challenge if she's overtly
flirtatious, showers a guy with sexual attention before he's shown any
interest, or makes it obvious that he can have her regardless of his
behavior. When a guy feels as if he hasn't earned your attention and
that you'll be impressed no matter what he says, it kills his attraction.
If he feels as if he could say or do whatever he wants, be as rude or
obnoxious as he wants, and still get your attention no matter how he
behaves, his attraction slowly dwindles. To remain attracted, he wants

to see that you have high standards and to prove himself as being capable of living up to them.

Paradoxically, a woman who comes across as completely uninterested also isn't a perceived challenge. A popular piece of dating wisdom advises women to pretend as though you couldn't care less. This. Does. Not. Work. Acting uninterested can actually just take you off his radar entirely. If you appear aloof, standoffish, unfriendly, and difficult, most men won't risk approaching you for fear of rejection. People are only motivated to take action on goals they think are attainable. Playing the ice queen never fails to intimidate every man in the room. This isn't a good thing if you are looking to make a connection.

Perceived value

Perceived value is the crucial element that makes a woman more than just a challenge. A woman who possesses perceived value is a woman of high value who's successfully managed to convey to a guy what she's all about.

The high-value woman demonstrates to a man that being with her is going to give him experiences that he could never have alone (or even with any other woman). Ultimately, whenever a man commits to a relationship it's because he realizes that being with this one special woman is infinitely more fulfilling than being single ever could be. A hundred random women can never compete with the power of the one woman who has made herself unique in his eyes.

The high-value woman is more than merely challenging, because she has a life that a man wants to be a part of. She has her own passions. She derives her self-esteem internally and doesn't rely on validation from a man in order to feel good about herself. She thinks and acts independently. A high-value woman has a world for him to explore, made up of friends, amazing experiences, fulfilling work, things that he aspires to have in his own life.

Connection

I mentioned the importance of connection earlier and the role it plays in the kinds of meaningful conversations that lead to first dates and beyond.

Connection is what makes someone realize he can be in his partner's company for hours on end. Passion is no substitution for connection, and sexual desire won't keep him hooked on your personality over the years. When we share that connection, just hanging out and watching a film seems exciting; we simply enjoy being in the other person's company. Connection requires us to be interested in someone's life, values, and standards. It's important to show on some level that we understand and can relate. So much of what we have discussed so far has been focused on your behavior and your value, and of course that is what this book is mainly about. However, I come back to the issue of connection time and again because it is the *exchange* of intimacies and experiences, not simply the offer of them, that creates a lasting relationship.

The Myth of Playing Hard-to-Get

Playing hard-to-get is one of the worst tactics for attracting men in the long term, primarily because that's all it is—a tactic. Pretending to be aloof, uninterested, or always too busy, the hard-to-get woman is play-acting. She makes herself seem like a scarce commodity to encourage the guy to chase her; when he finally gets what he wants, he's quickly bored and starts looking for another challenge. The attraction is built around the chase, instead of her. It's like dangling a string just out of reach of a cat. The cat goes crazy trying to grab the string, but when you finally drop the string, the cat loses interest.

When a woman relies on creating attraction using just the thrill of the chase, she finds herself pursued by only the most undiscerning, shamelessly persistent type of guys. These are the same guys who give up all dignity and self-respect just to get laid. Unlike a hard-to-get woman, a high-value woman *knows* that she is a challenge. She knows that she has high standards for the people she wants in her life, she doesn't have to fake the challenge. She is the woman a guy goes crazy for, the one who makes him realize that he has to raise his game to keep her.

Furthermore, a high-value woman can communicate her standards to a guy while also showing that she is interested in him. Having and communicating your standards is not about being hard to get, but about showing that only the guys who give you the most respect and investment of time and energy can get you.

A man feels deeply attracted when a high-value woman chooses him. Every man wants to feel that he has won his dream girl, and that something special about him caused her to choose him above every other guy in the world.

The bottom line is this: a guy wants a girl he feels no one else can get, not one he feels he can't get.

The Formula in Action

Some people are naturally better at certain parts of the process of creating attraction than others. One woman might be great at displaying her sexuality, so she has no problem creating visual chemistry and perceived challenge, yet she may struggle with making connection. She keeps everything hot, sexy, and superficial, so while inflaming his physical desire, she never makes her guy interested in who she is in everyday life.

Another woman might excel at both displaying her value and making a connection, and have a half dozen guys who love her for who she is, which is like a sister. This woman falls down when it comes to creating visual chemistry or perceived challenge.

The most effective combination is when all of these attributes are working in concert. The degree or weight of each one will vary from woman to woman, and that's okay. What makes you special is your individuality. But that doesn't change the necessity of being aware of each of these important character traits and learning how to leverage them in your favor.

11

A Word About Insecurity

We touched on this subject earlier in the book, but I feel it is important enough to bring up again in another context.

It's one thing to understand the formula for ultimate attraction, another to accept that it can truly work for you. Once a woman at one of my seminars laughed out loud when I suggested that any woman can create attraction with a first-rate guy.

I know that it's a challenge to dismiss your insecurities. There is always some aspect of yourself you worry about, whether it is physical—your shape, your height, your imperfect teeth, your slightly crooked nose, your oddly shaped ears, your thighs, your knees, that scar, that birthmark, that mole—or something deeper, like where you're from, your educational background, your health history, or any number of life experiences. (By the way, men fret about all these things too!)

You worry that after you've gone to all the work of building a fascinating social circle, finding and meeting a number of guys, creating connection through a fantastic conversation with one guy, playfully trading numbers, arranging a promising meet-up, now what? What happens when he gets a good look at you in broad daylight? When he realizes you're actually a good two inches taller than he is? When he sees you naked? Then what?

Back when I was in school a girl I liked once offered this completely unsolicited opinion: "You look really ugly when you smile." I'd been trying to appear friendlier and more approachable, having just read a book about body language that claimed smiling improves your looks. I still remember how devastated I felt.

But from this painful exchange—I really liked that girl—I learned a valuable lesson: one person doesn't hold the world's opinion. To fail to realize this is to allow one insensitive or hurtful comment to stick with you for years, festering as wounds sometimes do, and creating a belief about yourself based on nothing more than an offhand or even mean-spirited comment by someone who probably didn't realize that what they were saying might deeply offend you.

Indeed, a lot of us still carry insecurities today based on stupid comments made many years ago. We have a terrible tendency in life to focus only on our critics, those people who say the worst about us or those who react to us negatively. We cannot control someone else's response to us, but we can control our response to them.

A Golden Principle for Dealing with Insecurity

One of the most important lessons to learn about human dynamics is that first reactions don't count, because they are the least important. There are three things going on that contribute to someone's initial reaction to you:

1. Their previously held belief system and experiences. These things have nothing to do with you. (Maybe their last girlfriend had the same haircut, or you remind them of a teacher they hated in college . . . it could be anything.)

2. Their current mood—are they having a good day or a bad day? A bad day might make someone predisposed to shutting you out.

3. You.

So you are only one of three elements that influence someone's response. Since there is no way to know or measure what that implies, it is best to not pay too much attention to it. What does matter is *your* reaction to theirs.

Let's say you're six feet three inches tall and used to feeling awkward about being taller than most men. The next time someone says, "My god, you're tall!" instead of feeling self-conscious and apologetic, you can decide to appear comfortable and confident, and totally own it by saying, "I know, it's great. I can see everything from up here." Seeing that you are unaffected by the comment, the guy now perceives what may have been a negative attribute as a positive one.

When we own even our imperfections, our insecurities lose their power over us.

Everyone Has Baggage and Why It Doesn't Matter

The longer we live, the fuller our lives become. We sometimes convince ourselves that our history will turn off a potential partner. In the same way that we may feel insecure about our looks, we may feel embarrassed and uncertain about some of the stories that make up who we are. Not only is this unnecessary, but it is our past experiences that help create depth of character. The only regret or turnoff is bitterness. The rest is the stuff of life.

Why your age doesn't matter

There's no such thing as a perfect age. At twenty-one, you worry that a thirty-year-old guy is going to see you as inexperienced and immature. At forty-one, you worry that a guy will see you as over the hill. The reality is that where attraction is concerned, age rarely matters.

Remember, attraction is emotional, not logical. Some guys will say they're only into younger women, or older women, but what they think they want doesn't matter. I've known many guys who've married women nowhere near the age range they claimed they wanted.

Whatever our age, we have to learn to sell it as a strength. Any age can be used to your advantage. If you're twenty-one and feel immature and unworldly, you can play up your curiosity, which will give a guy the chance to show you the world and watch you grow. If you're older, you can play two cards: you bring a level of maturity and knowledge of the world and life (and sex, by the way) that a guy might not be able to get with a younger women, while also demonstrating youthful qualities like a desire for fun and adventure. This is a powerful and sexy combination of traits. Men aren't attracted to young women, they are attracted to youthfulness. Youth is something we do, not something we are.

When I was in my twenties, I once dated a women in her late thirties, and before we started dating her attitude toward me was "Not another one of those ridiculous young guys. I've got more of those coming after me than I know what do to with!" Then, when I finally had her attention, she teased me by saying, "I'm not so sure you can handle me." She was not my usual type, but she created attraction by treating her own age as a positive. She convinced me that she wasn't quite sure I was enough for her. She flipped the script!

Why your past relationships don't matter

Maybe you've had a string of relationships that didn't work out. Maybe you stick with a guy for a year or two, then for one reason or another, you both move on. Maybe you've been married and divorced—maybe even more than once.

Guys care about the details of your past a lot less than most women imagine. They're concerned much less about where you've been than about what your past may have taught you along the way and where you are going. What guys do respond negatively to is an embittered or cynical attitude, one that tells him that you are not yet emotionally detached from another guy or relationship. The important thing is to move forward with hope and optimism. The fact that your exboyfriend cheated on you means less to a new guy than your constant grumbling about how all men are cheaters.

Let the past go. When we're terrified of screwing up or getting hurt, we can cripple ourselves and our potential new relationship from the start.

Why being a single mom doesn't matter

A lot of women reel off statistics to me about single mothers and share many depressing anecdotes about shallow guys who flee the moment they hear a woman has a kid at home. I don't deny that these guys exist. But remember, statistics don't matter to the individual. You only need to meet one great guy who thinks you're amazing, regardless of who you're whipping up mac 'n' cheese for at home. Besides, why would you even begin to be interested in a man who can't appreciate how awesome children are and how the fact that you are a mother might add depth to your connection.

During a seminar I coached in Los Angeles, we did the usual part of the course where my clients put the lessons of the day into practice by going out and meeting guys. One woman was a single mom, and rather than being worried that no guy would want to date a woman with kids, she used her situation to flirt.

I heard her say to one guy, "Your dimples look like my daughter's. They are so cute." She was totally unfazed. Here was a woman talking about her kids, but doing it in a way that made it an entirely positive opening, precluding a negative response from the guy. She was a single mom, fun to be around, sexy, successful, and someone with a life. Her attitude told him from the outset that he might be lucky enough to share it with her.

When we're attracted to someone who might not fit our profile of the perfect partner, it's because that person displays qualities that make them attractive, and might also defy a stereotype in the bargain. When that happens—and it does all the time—all your preconceived notions about who is your type go out the window. In that moment, the only thing you feel is attraction. Attraction has its own power that goes beyond arbitrary characteristics.

The Truth About Imperfections

Beauty really is in the eye of the beholder. If we are comfortable with our imperfections, and see them as an intriguing part of the whole of who we are, then a guy will see them in the same way. Once he's attracted to you, your imperfections become not just irrelevant, but cherished.

Men and women are alike in this way: we're all looking for someone with a unique combination of qualities that make him or her like no other. When a guy discovers a woman like this, her superficial imperfections have no importance. No man has ever met a woman who makes him melt and then thought, Wow, she's the perfect woman for me. If only her hips were a little narrower and teeth a little straighter. Ah well, never mind, let's move on.

We all know someone who is not objectively good-looking but who nevertheless commands whatever room she enters. At a party, she's surrounded by people clamoring for her attention. Everyone enjoys her company and seeks her approval. She's magnetic and she makes people laugh. She makes big gestures, isn't afraid to take up space, and makes people feel good in her company. She's comfortable in her own skin. We notice her not because of her looks, but because of her charisma. And charisma is the aggregate of all of the qualities in the formula, put together in a unique way to create your own unique brew of attraction.

TURN A LIABILITY INTO AN ASSET

I want to share how one amazing woman turned her insecurity around and it changed her life.

Go to **www.gettheguybook.com/insecurity**
Access code: **gtgbook**

12

The Art of Creating the Great Date

What do most of us do on a first date? You go to some middle-of-the-road restaurant for dinner, make some light conversation, try not to eat anything that's going to get stuck in your teeth, and after two hours feel no closer to this person with whom you were feeling so excited to spend time. You feel as if you're in a bad movie, because it all feels artificial and awkward. You don't really feel comfortable with the person you're sharing a meal with—hell, you may have had only one brief, cocktail-enhanced conversation with him and now you're suddenly spending an entire evening in his company, awkwardly sitting face-to-face.

Only after the waiter has brought the menu does it occur to you that you've signed up for three hours of impersonating someone on a date. Is there any sexual chemistry here, any way to establish connection? Who knows? Your main goal has been reduced to not saying something stupid.

Earlier, I made my position clear about formal dates. I don't even think we should call them dates. I prefer the term "meet-up," as in "I'm going to meet up with that guy I met at my cousin's birthday party."

It's Not You, It's the Date:
Why Dinner and a Movie Doesn't Work

We need to stop treating dates as if they were a big deal where we get dressed up and plot an entire, endless evening of that creaky cliché that features drinks, dinner, and a movie.

I'm not against a date that involves drinking, eating, or movie-going per se, but we need to start thinking casually. The old-school formal dinner date has so many drawbacks, it's a wonder that people have stuck with it for so long.

The standard formal date rarely works for a number of reasons:

It's uninspired

On a first date you want to show a guy what makes you different from anyone else. A dinner date is business as usual, so the occasion doesn't promise anything memorable. He's been on dozens of dinner dates. Make him know you are different.

There's a good chance that this bad idea was his idea. You can him help recover from his lack of imagination by challenging him to be more creative. Tell him you've been working so hard lately and are feeling the need for something out of the ordinary—it doesn't have to be complicated. Maybe you suggest taking a walk along the river or going to the new Harley dealership to look at motorcycles. Then you can follow up with a playful challenge: "If you've got any good ideas let me know!" In this way you're also subtly communicating your standards. You're not just any woman to be dropped on the drinks-and-dinner date assembly line.

Alternatively, you can invite him along to something you've already got planned. "A few friends and I are going to this book launch tomorrow. Come with us!" Even though the guy asked you out on the date, you can lead him around to what you want to do by offering him a better alternative. Don't worry that he's going to feel rejected because you turned down his suggestion. You haven't said no to the date, you've just shown that you're high value and confident enough to express a preference for what you'd like to do. Besides which, most guys offer the dinner date only because they are being lazy and think it's a safe bet. With a little prompting on your end, you show him that he needs to try harder.

You have little chance to be your best self

The formal dinner date usually requires you put on "nice" clothes to which you may not necessarily be accustomed, then sit directly opposite each other and try to make conversation. It conjures up that horrible job-interview atmosphere, in which both parties trade interview-style questions back and forth, then judge each other's performance. What's more, you don't have much of a chance to behave in a way that increases your value. Even going for a walk through the park with an ice cream cone offers more of a chance for spontaneity and allows for the opportunity to share the more appealing parts of yourself.

You have no opportunity for casual physical contact

Sitting opposite a guy doesn't encourage touching, which removes one avenue for building chemistry and connection. This is why you both feel awkward at the end of the date, and you're not sure whether to kiss. During the date, if you haven't become comfortable touching in a light, playful way that feels natural, the idea of kissing will feel as if you're going from zero to ninety miles per hour. A good date should feel as if your physical intimacy is progressing until the kiss feels inevitable.

It's not flexible

The dinner date generally has to last for a few hours, during which you're at the mercy of the rhythms of the meal. After the first course, no matter how bad it's going, it's unlikely that one of you will bail. If things are going well, you are forced into a static interaction rather than a dynamic one. You're imprisoned until the check arrives.

The success of a date has absolutely nothing to do with the amount of time you spend together. A great date can be a twenty-minute breakfast before work or a ten-hour day starting with a picnic and ending with stargazing in a field. What matters is the connection and chemistry you feel on the date. You also want to be left wanting more of each other, not feeling like you've just passed an endurance test. Doing something engaging and out of the ordinary gives you both the best chance to explore whether there is sexual chemistry worth pursuing.

The Great Date

Many of us try to simply get through the first date. It's like enduring a turbulent flight; we pray, just get me through this, just get me through this. We try to avoid having a bad date, instead of focusing on having a great date.

This is where building a life you love pays off. Remember how while you were busy finding guys and meeting guys, you were also building your social circle, which included exploring your interests and passions? You were making a life that excited you and would eventually excite your guy.

When your lifestyle is a full and a key part of who you are, you don't have to scratch your head wondering where to go on a first date.

You already have interesting activities and social events, so you can invite your guy to join in.

You can ask him to come to your regular happy hour, where he'll both meet your friends and also have a chance to see you as the most popular person in the room. If you're both really into wine, tell him he should come along to a wine tasting you're going to next week. If you're both into art, tell him about a new exhibit you are going to see and invite him along.

A date doesn't have to be the two of you going it alone in an intense one-on-one environment. It can also be about bringing a guy into your world and seeing how it goes. This way you're able to interact with him in a more natural way, as well as see how he gets along with your friends and whether he's able to share your interests. You'll get a chance to see what it would be like to hang out with this person in everyday life.

You don't need to surround yourself with your friends on your date, but the point is that a date doesn't have to be an enormous, stilted, time-consuming event that feels separate from your normal life. The women who attend my seminars who say they don't have time to date obviously don't mean they don't have time for love. What they mean is they don't have time for a weekly or biweekly extravaganza, where they spend a few days prior to the date worrying about the perfect restaurant, stressing about the conversation, then an hour and a half deciding what to wear and putting on their makeup.

When we adopt a more casual mindset, it's much easier to imagine meeting up with a person we like. If you're having a busy, stressful week and you don't want to spend a whole evening on a date, then don't! Remember, longer dates don't equal better dates. The only purpose of a date is to connect with a guy to see whether he's someone with whom you want to spend more time and someone who lives up to your standards.

Where, then, might a great date take place? The zoo. An art

gallery. A food festival. Go bike riding or hiking. Fly a kite on the beach. Have a picnic in the park. Take in some local tourist attraction that you've wanted to see: How many New Yorkers make a point of going to the top of the Empire State Building?

What matters most isn't where we go or what we do, but that we choose a setting where we have the best chance to create a memorable date. A date should be a preview of how fun and intriguing life with you will be.

When He's Leading the Way

Sometimes you've found yourself a man-with-a-plan, and there's going to be no way to dissuade him from the deadly drinks-dinner-movie date. If there's no way around it, do your best to create great conversation using the techniques discussed in part one. At some point, however, if the first few dates go well, even the guy who likes to arrange the dates will be turned on by the idea of a woman who takes the reins and shows him something new.

During a busy week, one in which you don't have time for a full-blown date, text him and say, "Listen, I'm having a tough week but it would be great to catch up. How about we grab an ice cream at this place near my office after work? You have to try their salted caramel sundae!" Now it's not a big deal that you've arranged the date, because you've arranged it around the fact that the place has great ice cream. And the great thing is that this date is so casual that it doesn't have to last more than thirty minutes, and you can do it on the way home from work. Dating has to become a part of our lifestyle, not something completely separate from it.

The Golden Rules of the Great Date

The most important part of any date is not where you go, but what you do when you get there.

Connect, don't interview

I've already discussed the importance of being able to initiate and sustain an interesting, dynamic conversation. A date is all about seeking values rather than facts.

Let's say your meet-up is at an art gallery. It's tempting to converse about the pieces in front of you, and certainly that's part of the flow, but this is also an excellent opportunity to connect more deeply with your date. You might ask something like, "Which would you rather be: a great musician, a great painter, or a great writer?" Whichever he answers, ask him why. It's going to tell you something about him and what he values.

If the question sounds a little offbeat, that's good; this is the kind of conversation that makes a date memorable. Great conversation isn't rocket science, it's about creating an exchange of thoughts and feelings that make you stand apart from everyone else.

Good conversationalists get other people to open up and talk about what's meaningful to them. These quirky, speculative questions that are half playful and half serious have a way of allowing us insight into someone's true nature. Asking a guy, "What's your job?" tells us nothing compared to asking, "Why do you love your job?"

The advantage to this approach is that you find out the things you really want to know about someone much quicker than if you stuck with polite chitchat. Also, the quicker a guy feels like he can truly be himself around you, the more attracted he's going to be. Ask questions that might seem a bit cheeky: "What's the geekiest thing about you?" "What TV star do you have a secret crush on?" Getting him comfortable and laughing is much more important than trying to be cool. Every guy secretly loves when he can let someone into his weird little world, instead of having to hide it and pretend to be Mr. Smooth all the time. Be the girl who helps him to feel comfortable with who he really is.

Generate emotional spikes

Part of what makes a date memorable is how emotionally invested we find ourselves.

A great date should feel like a mini-adventure. You can draw the guy into anticipating the date by creating playful expectations. "If you don't like the dessert at this place, we're no longer friends!" you might say. Or if you're on a date to the zoo, you can take his arm and say, "I am terrified of anything with scales. You can only come if you promise to wrestle down any dangerous alligators with your bare hands." You've set up the dynamic that he has to protect you, and you can tease him by referring back to it, "I hope you've brought your tranquilizer gun. That crocodile just gave me a funny look, I might have to hide behind you." This behavior is silly and playful, but it gives you an excuse to joke around, make physical contact, and enjoy heightened emotion.

Another way to create emotionally memorable dates is to try something new together. Go skiing at a new place. Take a kayaking class. Sign up for an introductory cha-cha lesson or an Italian class—something that involves more investment than eating dinner and sitting in a movie theater.

Mind you, I love movies, and some of my best dates have been sitting at home watching a film, but at the beginning of a relationship the goal is to get under each other's skin. Sitting shoulder to shoulder in a movie theater may allow for some awkward hand-holding but doesn't give you much opportunity to create an emotional connection. It doesn't let you make easy physical contact, or create sexual tension and tease, or show off different sides of your personality and lifestyle; it hinders all of those things we want to do on a date that make us memorable.

A date should have a rhythm

If you're going out for a few hours or more, try hopping around to different venues. Go for a walk in the park, then to a coffee shop. Go check out the new exhibit at a museum, then find a place to shoot some pool. The date is more memorable because you're constantly changing the vibe; sometimes things are slow and intimate, sometimes fast and exciting.

Different kinds of dates allow us to share the different sides of our personalities. Variety helps us to feel closer to someone than if we simply keep going to that same bar, ordering the same drinks, then heading to the same restaurant every Friday night.

One date might show your sophistication. Another might show that you're sociable and have great friends. Another might be adventurous and show your spontaneity. Another might reveal your domestic side. The goal of dating, in addition to learning whether he meets your standards, is to show him that you are someone he could live and be comfortable with in a number of different circumstances. The fun part is, just when he thinks he's got you figured out, suddenly you show him another side he's never seen before.

Show him that you have a lifestyle
he wants to buy into

Another reason I'm against run-of-the-mill dates is because they make *us* seem run-of-the-mill. When a guy becomes deeply attracted to a woman, he's enticed not just by her, but also by the life she leads, and he wants to be part of it.

By putting a bit of extra thought into the time you spend with a guy, you show that you're the kind of person who puts extra thought into other areas of your life.

This, again, is the point of having a life you value and enjoy. Whether there's a guy in the picture or not, you're out there doing the things you enjoy. It's simply a bonus if your man of interest sees that you're passionate, love what you do, and have a strong identity. He would consider himself lucky to be able to share it with you.

Bring your best self

A first date isn't the place to moan or complain about your past. This guy that you're sharing a walk in the park with hasn't done anything to earn your rancor. We have to resolve to go into this thing with the attitude that whatever happened before is over; whatever bad experiences we've had in love before this moment, we're going to leave them behind.

Even if you've had a lousy day, are stressed at work, or are in a bad mood, leave it behind when you meet your date. Unless you possess the gift of being able to turn something potentially negative into a comedy skit, ask yourself, "What can I be excited about right now?" It doesn't have to be enormous. Maybe it's just the sunset or the turning leaves.

The one universal rule of attractive people is that they seem to be going somewhere. The person who meets us now is going to be a part of our future, and in that respect only one question matters: Does that future look compelling?

Guys Notice

In an earlier chapter I made the case for the general cluelessness of guys. Even though most guys are always looking out of the corner of their eye for a woman who might want to have sex with them, they really don't expect anyone to be interested in them. They're at the pub with their friends, drinking beer and playing darts, and they really don't have a clue to whether your look is meant for them. Maybe you're just looking at the clock.

That said, once you're dating a guy, he notices everything.

He's looking to see how well you treat your friends and whether you bitch about other people behind their backs. He's looking for whether you seem to get flustered easily or rattled at the first sign of teasing. He's looking to see if you are confident in your sexuality and believe in your own self-worth. He's looking to see whether you are superficial. He's looking to see your values.

He notices if you get crazy drunk and embarrass yourself, or if you are rude to the waiter. He notices whether you flirt with other guys or use your sexuality to get what you want, whether you get dramatic over little problems, whether you're easily angered and emotional, or whether it's tough to cajole you out of a bad mood.

Whether he's aware that he's evaluating you, he is. Women have been sold a myth that men never think about a relationship's potential on the first date and that they're only out to have a good time and get laid. (They are, but more on that in the next chapter.)

The truth is, guys are going through exactly the same thing you are. Guys categorize women fairly quickly. Before the first date is over a guy knows whether you're just a girl to date until someone he goes crazy for comes along. Or maybe you're just a woman he'd like to have sex with. He knows pretty quickly as well if you are the one he wants to take home to his family.

Sooner than you might imagine, he starts thinking things like: Would she get on well with my mother/my sister/my brothers/my cousins/my best friend? Will she be sociable with the people close to me? If I take her to a party, will she need to cling to me all night, or can I leave her to charm the room?

A scene in the TV show *Mad Men* captures this dynamic beautifully. Don Draper is on a business trip in Los Angeles, and he's brought along his kids and his secretary, Megan, to watch them while he's working. One night they're at a restaurant and one of the kids spills a milk shake. Immediately Don pulls himself up straight, a look of panic in his eyes. His ex-wife, Betty, would have lost her temper and pitched a fit and the evening would have been ruined. Instead, Megan grabs a bunch of napkins and starts mopping it up, completely blasé. She registers the horror on his face and says, "It's just a spill. It's no big deal." And in that moment, he falls in love with her.

This is why you always have to bring your best self to the table on a date. Always. If you've had a bad day and you're stressed, and you let it get to you, he's going to think that you're someone who is going to be a lot of work on a long-term basis. You have to be aware of how you come across; you might know that you're not normally in a bad mood, but he might assume you're like that all the time.

By the way, the first few dates are also your chance to notice everything about him. How much does he seem willing to integrate you into his life? If he's late, does he apologize or shrug it off? Does he lie about little things? If he doesn't take an interest in getting to know you, or doesn't make an effort to impress you, or doesn't express any interest in bringing you into his life, these are signals that he's not showing much investment. These things all add up, and you shouldn't ignore them in the early stages. If he does something you disagree with, call him on it. Tell him you think differently. He'll respect you more for being discerning.

We always have to have the abundance mindset. If a guy doesn't live up to your standards, there are a thousand others who will. You are on the date to see if he is what *you* are looking for. And when you bring your best self to the date, you help solidify your position of being the chooser because you become what he is looking for in return.

13

===

The Sex Talk (Part I)

When I first started my women's weekends, my groups were sometimes as small as eight. We huddled around a whiteboard in a tiny conference room. I avoided talking about sex. I wasn't being prudish, but rather cautious. I was terrified of offending every woman in the room. My role was offbeat enough already. I'd watched myself be labeled a "dating coach" on daytime TV and witnessed my mother awkwardly try to explain to her friends what her eldest son was now doing for a living. The last thing I wanted was to get a reputation as a sex guru.

For a while, I obeyed that old dinner party rule: keep conversation away from the big three topics—religion, sex, and politics. But I couldn't help thinking I wasn't being fair to my clients. Having promised to be completely open with women about how men think and what they want, how could I continue to gloss over sex, especially when men think about and want sex all the time? And I do mean *all the time*. There's an old joke that makes the point: the best time for a woman to have a serious conversation with a man is five minutes after they've had sex, because this is the only time he's not thinking about getting laid.

When Do You Sleep with Him?

In my experience the most persistent question on women's minds when it comes to dating and relationships is *How long should I wait until we have sex?*

In the early stages of a relationship, men and women generally take different roles when it comes to sex. Men are the pursuers and women the pursued. It is women, then, who make the ultimate decision about whether sex is going to happen.

Still, this doesn't mean a woman's sole power lies in her ability to allow or deny a man sex. Thousands of magazine articles are churned out every month telling you that the only way to get a guy to continue to pursue you is to withhold sex for a specific number of dates, or to not have sex until he has committed to a relationship, or other rules that provide no help in keeping a guy in the long term.

Most of the women I know seem to hold to the wait-three-dates rule, which is based on thinking something like this: "If I wait until after our third date, he'll see that I'm not as easy as those other slutty girls he dates. Then he'll realize that I'm someone he has to get serious about before anything is going to happen." This possesses a certain kind of logic, but it's another rule that misses the point. I know plenty of guys who will wait until after three dates for sex and still never commit.

It's not just a question of how long you make him wait for sex. Making him wait for an arbitrary length of time sets you on the course away from genuine connection and into pointless game playing, which never ends well.

While my personal philosophy is that you shouldn't make a policy of having sex on the first date (I am not saying that you should never have sex on the first date), my reservations have nothing to do with the fact that you haven't made him wait long enough. Making a guy wait for sex is not what keeps him interested in you.

The Emotional Hook Point

When the average guy goes out on a date, part of him always hopes to have sex at the end of it. He's pretty much hardwired this way. If he is on a date with you, he's already decided there is visual chemistry, and if he's decided there's visual chemistry, he's going to want sex with you. This doesn't make him a good or bad man, it's simply a fact.

It is a mistake to think there are two types of guys: nice guys interested in you for who you are and players who only want sex. No such dichotomy exists. A player is just more up front about his intentions, while the nice guy is playing a longer game but still wants to take you home and have his way with you.

In short, guys know they may not always get sex, but they're always hoping for it. Still, the notion that "men only want one thing" is only partially true. It is one thing they are sure to want, but it is not the only thing. In fact, men are just as receptive as you are to becoming deeply attached. When a guy becomes attracted to your personality and loves spending time in your company, when he sees you as someone special, someone he wants in his life, perhaps forever, it's because the two of you have established an emotional connection. Sex becomes a way to deepen that connection.

It matters not whether you've been on two dates or five dates, whether he's met your parents or you've met his buddies, or whether he keeps pressing you to sleep with him every time you meet. Sex should enter the relationship when the emotional connection has been made. I call this connection the emotional hook point.

When a guy reaches the emotional hook point, he will be thinking about you when he's watching a film with his buddies. He'll be thinking of calling you the moment he gets off work. He'll find a way to be in your neighborhood when it's not even remotely convenient. He'll go to sleep at night and wonder what you're doing. And that's usually when a guy thinks, Oh man, I think I've fallen for this girl—often a scary moment for him, especially if he thought he was enjoying his single life. In essence, he's been hooked.

This emotional connection is created through shared experience. This is more than simply spending time together on a few standard dates, but about doing things together that involve the possibility of gaining emotional investment. It's about the intensity of the experiences you share and conversations that you have.

This is why it's important to try to go on dates that allow for meaningful interactions rather than those dastardly dinner dates, where there's little opportunity to bond in a significant way. It's why it's important to have dates that involve sharing a new experience or doing something to which you both have a genuine connection (or through which you can make one).

The more meaningful time you spend with a guy, the greater the variety of experiences you have together, the greater the chance he'll reach an emotional hook point. Emotional connection is not *just* a function of time, however. Time may help, but time spent together does not in itself produce emotional connection.

Vacation romances can be powerful for this very reason. You can have intense shared experiences over a very concentrated period of time. Usually both people are out of their immediate environment, so they are sharing something new and exciting, maybe adventurous and out of the ordinary. What's more, this environment encourages people to open themselves up more, and so they reach the emotional hook point quicker.

To understand how to make an emotional connection, it's important to know what does not help you make one:

Passion is not the emotional hook point

You don't want to misconstrue wanting to tear each other's clothes off for having reached an emotional hook point. It may feel intensely emotional on your side, but a guy can feel a staggering amount of physical chemistry, yet still feel detached emotionally. His level of physical passion is not an indicator of his lasting attraction.

Being really into him is not the emotional hook point

When you really like someone it's important to avoid supposing there's an emotional connection on his side that might not yet exist. This is a recipe for unrequited love. It leads to a one-sided situation where we feel deep attraction for someone who doesn't share our emotional involvement. If you find yourself having endless conversations with your friends about why this new guy is always busy and can't make time for you, or how the relationship doesn't seem to be going anywhere, chances are it's because you've confused your swooning, emotionally intense feelings for him with mutual emotional connection that doesn't (yet) exist.

Sex itself is not the emotional hook point

It's not uncommon for a woman to suppose that since a guy is begging for sex, granting his wish is a way to create emotional connection. This may seem logical to the female mind, but sex doesn't work that way for men, who don't tend to form lasting attachments through sex. Even the nicest of guys can sleep with a woman and remain detached.

If a man doesn't feel any emotional connection with the woman he has sex with, it's easy for him to compartmentalize their interactions. He might genuinely like the woman he's sleeping with but still view her primarily as an enjoyable escape from the everyday realities of work and paying the bills.

If sex comes too quickly or too easily, a man may feel neither the interest nor the obligation to invest more significantly in getting to know you or getting closer to you. The part of him that's focused on sex hijacks his brain, and his sole mission becomes seducing you, rather than trying to connect on any deeper level. When sex becomes the focus it's more of a challenge for you to showcase your personality, making it much more difficult to establish an emotional connection.

SOMETIMES YOU HAVE TO JUST GET IT ON

Here is one scenario where you can sleep with a guy immediately and still make him feel like he's earned it.

Go to **www.gettheguybook.com/hookpoint**
Access code: **gtgbook**

The Biggest Male Anxiety About Sex

I fear I've painted a discouraging picture of the male mind, portraying men as little more than dogs who, once you've produced the treat of sex, are incapable of focusing on anything else. But it's not quite that simple. Even the kindest, most compassionate man, with three beloved sisters and a genuine appreciation of all women, seeks personal validation through sex. Much of his self-esteem is wrapped up in how attractive and sexually desirable he feels. On a primal level, it makes him feel like a man. It is the one thing he wants above everything else.

But the feeling of sexual validation doesn't just come from the sex act. Acquiring sex isn't so much about the action itself; rather, it's a signal that his fundamental need to be chosen has been met. What makes him feel truly validated is the knowledge that a woman could have had her pick of any guy in the room, but she chose him.

Every man secretly wants to feel as if only he could have possibly had sex with you. No other guy in the room could have gotten you. I realize this sounds a little needy, but the truth is that a man can be needy when it comes to sexual validation. He wants to feel that something about him pushed your buttons. He wants to believe that he turned you on in a way that made you choose him over anyone else.

If you take only one piece of truth away from this book, make it this: men appreciate physical contact that they have earned.

Unearned physical contact doesn't give a man sexual validation. Here's why: men suffer anxiety at the thought that they just had a woman anyone could have had. It's one of the reasons many men have disdain for women who are considered slutty or easy. When a guy thinks, What I just did, anyone could have done, he's not feeling good about himself.

Consider again the formula for attraction:

Visual Chemistry + Perceived Challenge + Perceived Value + Connection = Deep and Lasting Attraction

When it comes to sex, if a guy suspects that any other guy could have also gotten you into bed, your perceived value plummets in his eyes. He suspects that you have no firm standards. He doesn't feel as if he had to seduce you or charm you in any unique way. He hasn't had to *work* for you. He feels as though his only achievement was being present at the right time. What's more, if it all comes too easily, it also means there was no perceived challenge, which further kills his attraction.

How to Tell If He Just Wants Sex

Since all guys want sex, how do you tell when a guy is *only* out for sex? Even great guys will try for sex on the first or second date, so how do you spot the ones who don't plan on sticking around?

The first thing to notice is how he reacts to you denying him sex. If his reaction is too emotional, or angry, or upset, or he is too persistent about having to have sex right this minute, ditch him. A guy will react emotionally to being denied sex only if he plans on never having another date with you, or if he has his own emotional hangups. Either way, you don't need any part of it.

A good rule of thumb is to never punish a guy for wanting sex, but be concerned if he reacts badly to your denial. Denying a guy sex doesn't have to be done in a stern, formal way. You can say no without making him feel rejected. If you say to him: "You're really cute, but I don't move that fast," you are still throwing approval his way.

The guy who enjoys your company and wants to get to know you better will have no problem not having sex on a first, second, or third date. If he is truly interested in pursuing a relationship with you, he will wait until you are ready (within reason!). Mostly, he'll just need some sense of progression as the two of you get closer. If he's reached the emotional hook point with you, if you've become a woman like no other in his eyes, the actual sex can wait. He's confident it will happen eventually; whether it's tomorrow, next week, or next month, he knows it will happen. Your denial won't concern him if he feels a connection to you, especially one of value to him. Time with you becomes worth waiting for a physical relationship with you. This is a good reason for denying a guy sex on a first date; if nothing else, it allows you to see whether he plans on having another. Although he may wait two more dates for sex, at least then he'll value it differently.

How to Be an Unforgettable Woman

A sophisticated woman assumes that guys will desire her sexually, but she doesn't make that her value. A guy's basic urge to want to sleep with her doesn't dictate how she behaves. She engages with him on her own terms.

Suppose a guy rings you up at 10 p.m. and asks you to come over. A smart woman will know that a booty call is never the way to gain respect and help establish a genuine relationship. But just because he's called for one, that doesn't mean you chastise him for trying to have sex with you.

What you can do is to suggest an alternative. Say to him, "I'll tell you what, I'll come over in the morning and we'll have breakfast instead." Then bring some orange juice and croissants over to his place in the morning. Now you've turned what would have been a purely sexual situation into a connection situation. Sure, he might initially feel a little frustrated when he can't get you to come over at night, but a little frustration never hurt anyone.

All that matters for a guy is that he is kept excited. He doesn't mind if sex isn't in the cards right away if you are adding value to his life. As long as he still feels like he's in the game and that he's got something to look forward to, he doesn't mind waiting.

The unforgettable woman isn't worried about how her guy will feel when he's made to wait. If he's focused on sex, she's focused on expressing her value. This is the value of the casual dates mentioned earlier. When you do ordinary stuff, like cooking a meal together, walking down to a local coffee place, or even just hanging out together reading the Sunday paper or catching up on some work on your laptops, opportunities abound for both displaying your value and connecting emotionally.

I'm not suggesting that it's your job to bring meaning and value to a guy's life. Nor am I suggesting that you invest any time in a guy who doesn't meet your standards. The principle of reciprocity is always operational. Yes, you give first, but you expect something in return. Invest, and then test his reaction.

This still might sound both too exhausting and too risky; you might feel as though you don't want to waste time and energy on someone who isn't interested in anything serious. Actually, behaving this way saves you time. If the guy who wants you to come to his place at 10 p.m. won't take you up on your breakfast offer, and keeps pressing you to come over late at night, you'll know immediately that he isn't interested in investing more in the relationship. If someone proves to be unworthy of your investment, waste no further time with him and feel glad to have found out sooner rather than later.

All this said, if you want a meaningful, long-term relationship, bringing value to the table is what makes a guy want you for who you are. The woman who demonstrates value early on is the one who gets pursued beyond sex.

14

===

Stuck in the Friend Trap

My friend Laura is one of those women whose friends can't believe she is still single. She's got a job she likes, belongs to a running club, goes out salsa dancing a few times a month, travels the world a few times a year. She's pretty and lively and has a knack for drawing people out and making them feel good about themselves. She always seems to have a lot of attractive men around her. Laura's ability to meet so many new men is enviable, but it somehow never seems to result in any dates for herself. In fact, most of her time with these guys is spent talking about other women they are seeing. She is, essentially, one of the guys, but a better listener.

Laura keeps finding herself in the dreaded friend zone. Her new male friends may love her, but they're not *in* love with her.

Some women are gifted at becoming a guy's best friend. They have a seemingly endless supply of male friends with whom they can hang out. They spend lots of time connecting and making jokes, but like Laura's, the relationships never seem to go anywhere romantically.

This is because attraction requires more than just a connection. It also requires sexual tension and chemistry, which only come from being comfortable with our sexuality. As blind as guys can be to most body language, they're well attuned to the moves of a woman who is sexually confident.

What the "buddy girl" tends to do is make friends with a guy first, hoping a flame will spark and seduction will follow. But as long as you are firmly in the friend zone, it's hard for you to appear on his radar as a sexual partner. If your behavior was a mathematical equation, it would look something like this:

(Playfulness + Spontaneity + Connection)
– Sexuality = Friend Trap

Most of us have been there at some point in our love lives. We've met someone with whom we long to have a romantic relationship but who only sees us as a friend. And let's face it, the friend zone sucks.

If we find ourselves in this position repeatedly, it's because we are taking a wrong turn early in the relationship. It usually happens to people who are good at building rapport and connecting on a deep level with someone, yet fail to express their sexuality enough to be seen as something more than a friend. And so, while a guy sees one of these women as great company, that's the *only* way he sees her.

Somewhere along the way he failed to see you as sexual. Perhaps you were great at flirting and letting him see your sexy side at the party that first night. Then once you began seeing each other, you wanted to show him what a good, loyal, faithful companion you could be and wound up reminding him too much of his sister.

Or, you're so deliriously happy to have found this guy, you go overboard lavishing him with attention. It becomes clear to him that you're eager to be with him, regardless of how he behaves, and that he doesn't have to do any work at all to keep to you interested. In this case, he isn't perceiving you as either high value or a challenge.

It rarely feels good to be in the friend zone. You feel powerless and unloved. You get stuck in the position of hoping that something will happen; all the while he hooks up with other girls. He likes spending time with you, but he only sees you as his buddy, as someone he can hang out with and confide in, but not as a romantic partner. And you can't understand why. You know you would be great for him. And what's worse, it stops you from meeting anyone else, because you don't want to jeopardize your chances with him, and your focus is only on him. Every time he's single, you think there might be an opportunity for him to notice you. You hope that eventually he'll just realize that you've been there all along.

No one can blame you for holding out hope that one day the lightbulb will go on over his heart and he'll realize you've been the one for him all along. You could name ten Hollywood movies with the exact same plot: Guy and girl are friends for years. They sleep with other people, never realizing that they are totally right for each other. After years and years of holding back, one of them (usually the guy) dramatically runs to the girl at the last possible moment (due to last-minute plot contrivances usually involving getting on an airplane) and he confesses how he has always loved her, how he realizes she is totally and completely the one for him, and how he just wants to spend the rest of his life with her.

I'm here to tell you that this is the stuff of movies; the only time I can remember that Hollywood got it right was the famous scene from *When Harry Met Sally* in which Harry and Sally are having a relaxed lunch at Katz's Delicatessen. They are still just friends at this point, and Harry is talking about his sex life. He argues that he is always able to sexually satisfy a woman. Sally disagrees. She maintains that all women now and then have to fake orgasms, and that Harry would never be able to tell the difference between a real and a fake one. When Harry shakes his head cynically and assures her that he could, Sally responds in the most shocking way possible. In order to prove her point, she begins to close her eyes, she gently moans, breathing heavier and heavier, she then moans louder, and louder still, until finally she's screaming at the top of her voice "Oh God, yes! YES!

YES!" and fakes an entire orgasm from beginning to climax in the middle of the diner.

When Sally fakes the orgasm, Harry sees this person, whom he has always considered as just a friend, in a sexual way in which he has never seen her before. Although this is an exaggerated example, it shows how a woman can suddenly show a man a side of her personality that he never even thought about. Suddenly, in that moment, Sally looks like a sexual goddess.

This is when Harry *really* meets Sally.

How to Get Out of the Dreaded Friend Zone

If you want to have a guy friend, that's great. There's nothing wrong with having a primarily male social network (guys can introduce you to other guys) or a male best friend. But if you want to stop getting stuck in the friend zone with men you desire, and with whom you can imagine a long and happy romantic future, the best thing to do is either meet someone new or do something new. Here are some pointers to help you shift his attitude toward you.

Don't become his relationship coach

A guy friend is probably going to talk to you about other women he thinks are hot, or other women he's seeing or dating. He may also feel free to ogle other women in front of you. If you still possessed any doubts about whether the two of you were more than friends, this clinches it. The more you play therapist, talking through all of his relationship issues with other women, the further down the buddy trail you're headed. The trick is not to indulge him. Don't let him go on about some girl he's into, don't give him advice or try to gently tell him what to do. Avoid the topic altogether. You don't want to hear about it.

If you get stuck as his relationship coach, it leaves you no room to flirt and show off your own qualities. Being his coach might make you feel closer to him. It may make you feel as if your relationship is more "authentic" and honest, but getting close doesn't necessarily equal more attraction.

Be willing to disagree with him

When we like someone, our impulse is to get along in order to build rapport. We're desperate to find some common ground. This may lead you to say you agree with his opinions, even if you don't. Or you won't challenge him on something about which you'd normally cause a ruckus, because you don't want to make waves. You're bending to accommodate him to show him how well you fit together instead of just sticking to your own opinions and standards, which is the kind of thing friends do—see each other's point of view, agree to disagree, build consensus. One of the ways to make sure you don't slip into the friend zone is to be willing to challenge him on things.

It sounds counterintuitive, but one way to be more attractive is to break rapport with a guy by disagreeing with him. A guy doesn't want a yes-woman who agrees with everything he says. I don't recommend you ever fake this, but if he says something that's out of step with your values, or he says he likes a movie, book, or band that you can't stand, be willing to cause a little trouble.

If he's moaning and groaning a lot about his workload or his favorite team's recent losing streak, you can say, "I could never be with you—you're way too much work." This is a way of playfully communicating your standards. You can also say this if he ever jokes about the idea of the two of you being together. In fact, if he ever jokes about it, say, "Yeah, we'd never work, I'm way too cool for you."

Bear in mind that for this to work you cannot say it seriously. The tone always has to be a bit cheeky, like you're only playing with the idea of being together. You're not remotely serious.

Do you see what's happening here? You're both putting the idea of a relationship in his head, while also taking it away. This is an elegant way of communicating high value to a guy, because now you've suggested he's going to have to live up to your standards. This is key for long-term attraction. As we've established, a man always wants to feel that the woman he's with is forcing him to raise his game. He wants to feel ever so slightly like he has to do more to keep up with her.

The relevance of breaking rapport is not to disagree for the sake of it. It's to convey that however much you might be into him you're not going to agree with everything he says. It's a way of communicating both certainty and independence. It shows that you have your own opinions, even on things as trivial as movies. Paradoxically, disagreeing can create more attraction than agreeing for the sake of getting along. When you disagree on some things, it makes your bond much stronger when you eventually find common ground.

Let him know what's off limits

If he persists being a guy friend and not your boyfriend, make it clear to him that certain things are off limits. There are certain perks of being in a relationship with you that he's not entitled to because you're only friends. Being able to see you naked, or how sexy you are in the bedroom, or what kind of underwear you own—these things are reserved for the man with whom you're in a romantic relationship. Again, don't chide him or lecture him, just playfully let him know there are certain wonders behind the velvet curtain that he could partake of, were the two of you a couple.

If you're having a conversation about sex, never be explicit, just hint at how amazing you are in that arena and let him imagine the rest.

If he asks you a personal question about it, say in a teasing manner, "I don't reveal my secrets to just anyone." Now you are showing him that there is a level of closeness he can't get by just being friends with you. It implies both that you are high value and that you have hidden depths.

Make him have sexual thoughts about you

Being able to convey her sexuality is one of the traits of a desirable woman. This is what makes a guy able to picture himself kissing you, wanting to touch and be sexual with you. If you want out of the friend zone, it's important to get comfortable with the idea of a guy thinking about having sex with you. I realize this sounds fairly basic, but you might be surprised how many women, in their eagerness to show that they're kind, smart, honest, and trustworthy, lose sight of this basic requirement of romance.

Even if he likes you, he may find it hard to think of you as a romantic partner because he can't picture what being physically intimate with you will be like.

When a guy is looking at you romantically, he's always wondering what sex is like with you, even before the first date. A guy often secretly wants to feel that you have a really naughty side that he's not yet allowed to see, but that has the potential to emerge with him. This is why it's so important that he views you as sexual early on. You might be thinking, Well, he'll see what a sex fiend I am once he's in a relationship with me, but it doesn't work that way.

As we mentioned before, the early stages of courtship should be a preview for the rest of the relationship. A guy always wants to see an indication of the traits he's looking for early on.

There are several ways to display your sexual nature without coming on to him in a way that's overly forward. Dancing with a guy is a great way for him to notice your sexuality; when he sees you enjoy moving your body and being in the moment, he can't help feeling closer to you physically. Another way is to let him know that you have sexual thoughts. You never want to just stride up to a guy and tell him you want to have sex with him. After he gets over the shock, he'll usually feel intimidated. You also don't want to outright say to him, "You're so sexy"; this might be something you say in a relationship or in bed, but saying it early on feels like too much.

Instead of telling him outright that he's sexy, tell him that something he *does* is sexy. For example, if a guy is wearing a new leather jacket, say, "Wow, that jacket is sexy" or "Hey! You know I can't resist guys in leather jackets. Take that off right now."

If he's wearing a new aftershave and you say, "Oh my, I can't resist that smell on a guy," you're making it about the aftershave, not about him personally.

Even in general conversation when you use phrases like, "I can't resist that . . ." or "It turns me on when . . ." or "It's so sexy when . . . ," you are communicating your sexual desires. This is the kind of language that distinguishes a romance from a friendship.

If you're confident enough, you can be sexual moments after you meet a guy. You don't have to wait. You could be standing next to a guy at a social function and say, "I can't stand next to you. I have a fetish for guys who wear scarves." It's a silly line, but it establishes from your first interaction that the two of you are never going to be just friends.

Let's take a closer look at one of the lines above: "Hey! You know I can't resist guys in leather jackets. Take that off right now."

This line (and every similar line about how something drives you crazy and he must stop immediately or suffer the consequences) serves to both offer a compliment and immediately rescind it. You're saying, in essence, "You turn me on, but you're not allowed to." You're saying, "I'm attracted to you, but I'm not sure I should be." You're telling him that you find him sexy in a leather jacket, but you are also communicating that by being sexy he is breaking the rules.

So of course, what does he want to do?

Break the rules.

Now, he's going to want to turn you on more, because you've prohibited it. Moments ago he was just standing there minding his own business, and now he's determined that you continue to see him in a sexual light. You've started a game, which he wasn't expecting. When you tease him in this way, you are conveying your interest but also throwing enough challenges in his path that he wants to keep your interest going.

Don't come running every time he calls

Often when we're stuck in a "just friends" situation with someone we're attracted to, we'll drop everything we're doing just to be closer, hoping that maybe one day they'll notice we're there and fall in love. But proximity isn't attraction.

When you overinvest in a guy too quickly, it extinguishes any initial attraction he may have felt for you. By making it clear that you have nothing better going on in your life than being with him, you never give him the chance to see what he's missing when you're not around. It's a version of the country-western song lyrics: "How can I miss you when you won't go away?"

In the early stages of a relationship, a guy wants to see that you have standards and commitments, neither of which you're going to compromise for anyone. If he feels as if you'll come running anytime he calls, it's easy to end up as the woman he calls up to make himself feel good or to boost his ego, but not someone for whom he feels attraction.

I know this is easier said than done. When we're attracted to someone, the impulse to compromise our own standards is great. One friend described being in love as like being caught in a riptide. No matter how much you resist, you can't seem to help yourself. He doesn't show you the same attention you show him? That's okay! I give up every minute of my spare time to be at his beck and call? Sure!

Friends? Who needs friends, when I've found the man of my dreams! But this kind of behavior never works in your favor; slowly but surely your value drops in his eyes, and whatever attraction he may have once felt for you diminishes.

I'm not advocating playing hard-to-get, but a guy should only get back what he invests.

Get physical

If *you* want to be the one to choose who is going to be a friend and who is going to be something more, you must get comfortable touching people. Touching a guy in conversation should always be seamless and graceful. It shouldn't feel like something awkward or unusual, it should feel like something you do normally.

Resolve to become more tactile with everyone. In the same way that we have to become more sociable with everyone, we also have to become more comfortable with using touch in everyday conversation. If you're uncomfortable with touching, start practicing with everyone in your life.

Hug your friends when you greet them or when you're saying good-bye. Kiss a guy on the cheek when you greet him. If you do it with everyone in the group, people will see your confidence and follow suit.

Learning to reach out to people in this way will eventually dissolve your barriers and make you feel more open to people. We all know that friend who lights up the room with their warmth. They instantly make everyone feel close to them by being affectionate not with just one person, but with everyone.

Do this, and the next time you touch a guy to flirt with him, it's not going to seem weird or unnatural, it's just going to seem like a natural extension of your personality. This is why I recommend you flirt with everyone, even women. Why? Because this gets you to take yourself less seriously all the time. And when you bump into that guy you find attractive, you don't feel like you have to switch suddenly into flirting mode.

One great way to make touch easier in a first conversation is to stand next to someone, instead of face-to-face. (Standing side by side also gives the impression that you could walk away at any time, that you're still deciding whether to commit to the conversation.) When you stand next to someone, your arms might be touching and it still feels perfectly natural. It allows you to touch the back of his arm and point out something across the room or say, "Come meet my friends."

When it comes to touching someone you know better, with whom you might be entering the friend zone, you can be a little bolder. Give him a short shoulder massage, or a more intimate, longer hug. If you notice his aftershave or shampoo, you can lean in and smell him (lightly touch the back of his arm to pull yourself toward him).

All of these instances of touch help create connection and intimacy, and give him an excuse to get close to you. In touching a guy briefly and frequently, you're telling him it's okay to make a move. The major reason a guy might not kiss you on a first date is that he lacks the chance or reason to get close to you. There's always that moment near the end of the date where the conversation dies and the woman is thinking, Just do it. Just kiss me already! Meanwhile he's thinking, I want to kiss her, but how do I get over there? She's like eight hundred feet away. Do I pretend there's a bug on her shoulder and lean forward to brush it off? Do I pretend to accidentally trip and fall into her lips?

When you take the lead and make touch feel more natural, he's going to find it easier to reciprocate. Building up to a kiss is much easier if he already feels comfortable with being physically close and touching. You're giving him permission, but letting him make the move.

TO TOUCH OR NOT TO TOUCH

Watch me and an audience member demonstrate the art of suggestive touching.

Go to **www.gettheguybook.com/touch**
Access code: **gtgbook**

Other Traps

There are many ways a promising relationship that gets off the ground well enough nevertheless finds itself stalling out and plunging to the ground. Here are some of those scenarios.

(Femininity + Sexuality) – Connection = Sex Object Trap

Some women, convinced that the way to a man's heart is through his groin, focus on their sexiness, and some women naturally ooze sexuality. The way they walk across a room, the way they apply lipstick, the way they touch a man conveys one thing and one thing only. These women are usually naturals when it comes to creating some quick and raging chemistry. A guy will want to have sex with her immediately (Hey, is there anyone in the guest bathroom?).

Without playfulness, however, the woman stuck in the sex object trap comes across as merely a seductress. Without integrity and independence, she comes across as someone who is sexual but doesn't have any significant standards.

A guy might get addicted to this sexual energy, but once that wears off—and eventually it does wear off—he loses interest, because he can't see himself living with her on a long-term basis. She has demonstrated her sexual value, but not her ability to connect with and understand him on any deeper level. He may keep calling her for sex, but eventually he'll find someone who possesses all the traits that attract him, and she'll never hear from him again.

(Certainty + Independence + Connection) – Femininity – Playfulness = Serious Type Trap

Many high-powered women who've achieved a great deal, who stride through the world in seven-league boots, taking names and kicking ass, sometimes struggle to season their great confidence, certainty, independence, and competence with a pinch of femininity and playfulness.

It's not as if they've completely shut themselves off from those other qualities that are necessary to create attraction in a guy, but they may be rusty from lack of use. The persona of a strong, successful woman that a woman needs to inhabit in working life undoubtedly requires dialing down her cheeky, flirty, womanly side.

Every guy she meets takes her seriously. There's no risk of her falling into the sex object trap, or perhaps even the friend trap. Men who are equally successful want to hire her, and men who are less successful want to take a seminar taught by her, but none of them want to develop a romantic relationship with her.

There's no intrinsic conflict between being a strong, certain woman and one who embraces her femininity and sweetness, but like everything, getting all of those traits up and running at the same time takes practice.

The Just-Be-Yourself Trap

I don't have an equation for this trap, which is the trickiest one of them all.

In the early stages of a relationship, a man becomes attracted when he glimpses in you all of the traits that make a desirable, high-value woman. I'm sure there are some days when behaving in ways that convey that high value to others feels like learning one of those sports, like tennis or skiing, that requires you to perform about sixteen different moves at the same time.

For some, if not most, of you, embracing some of these traits will feel initially uncomfortable. It may feel incredibly out of character to be sexual if you are someone who is not used to expressing that side of yourself. It may be difficult being playful if you are used to being sensible. It may be hard to be spontaneous because spontaneity makes you anxious. Maybe you have a habit of falling head over heels with a guy in the first half hour after you've met him, and so conveying certainty and standards is a struggle.

This can be frustrating. It may make you want to quit. After a night at an office party, or a barbecue, or an art opening, after which you're convinced you made a fool out of yourself trying to exhibit traits you're convinced you don't possess, you may confide your woes to a friend and she will say, inevitably, "You don't have to change a single thing. Just be yourself and it will be fine."

This is where our friend can be our worst enemy.

The advice to forget everything you've learned and to just be yourself doesn't even make much sense. Who is to say what our real self really is? Do you even know? I don't. The great philosophers of the world all seem to go to their graves never having found a definitive answer.

What if I've suggested some things in this book that you've enjoyed doing? Meeting and mingling with new guys, striking up great conversations, becoming a more tactile person. Are you going against your "true" self because you're now more practiced at being outgoing and playful?

The habits, both good and bad, that we may have fallen into over the years do not constitute who we are. We are simply used to being that way. We're used to going out with a friend, buying a drink, and huddling with her in the corner, complaining that there are no good men out there. We're used to going on dinner dates to dull restaurants and grinding through boring conversations about where we work and how long our commute is. We're used to sleeping with a guy on the third date because we read in a magazine about the wait-three-dates rule.

This isn't who we are.

Even a woman who's shy in public still sings in the car when she hears her favorite song. She has a side to her that others rarely see, a side that is silly, playful, and spontaneous. Likewise, there are strong, certain women who go nuts for expensive French lingerie, and playful, spontaneous women who've disciplined themselves to meditate for thirty minutes every morning for their entire adult life. Do all of their friends know this about them? Not likely.

Often, when people advise "just be yourself," it's a way of saying don't grow and change. What's more, friends offer this advice when just being yourself has left you miserable and lonely. What they are really telling you is to stick with what you know, to stay with what is comfortable. And what I am telling you is that the new and improved you is *you*. You are not *changing* who you are, you are *becoming* who you are.

15

===

Why Hasn't He Called?

You had a great time. You thought everything was going so well. You talked easily. He told you a secret or two. He held your hand as you strolled to the car. You made an impromptu stop for ice cream. You talked until two. You could have easily slept together. He remembered the name of your cat as he said his good-byes. You had a great time! You thought everything was going so well.

Suddenly, radio silence. The phone doesn't ring all week. Maybe you break down and call him and leave a message. But he doesn't call you back.

Why is the guy not calling you back?

The Reasons You Think He's Not Calling Are Not the Real Reasons

===

Throughout my years of coaching I've discovered that the reasons men *really* don't call women back are completely different from the reasons women generally suppose. These are some of the most common fallacies.

He didn't call me back because he's intimidated by me

This is one of the most common misinterpretations. I've met and worked with many successful women who are so fond of this reason, they trot it out before the first date has even occurred. "Just watch," a woman who attended one of my seminars said after she'd traded numbers and made a date with a guy she'd met at a party. "He'll be too intimidated by me to make this work."

Successful women have a habit of assuming that a guy can't handle their level of achievement, or that a guy is always turned off by a woman more advanced in her career than he is. But the truth is, unless a woman behaves on a date as she does in a business meeting, or aggressively interrogates a guy under the guise of conversation, most of the time men are intrigued and even turned on by a successful woman, especially one who also displays a degree of femininity, playfulness, spontaneity, and sexuality.

He didn't call me back because I'm not good-looking enough

If a guy has been on a date with you, he's already decided that he likes what he sees. One of the main reasons he asked you out in the first place is that there was visual chemistry. Unless he was wearing a blindfold on the day you met, he already thinks you're good-looking enough.

But it is possible that he went on the date without feeling any sexual chemistry, hoping some might develop. A guy wants to feel as if he can imagine having wild sex with you, which is easy to do with a girl who laughs and teases him, who's passionate and seems comfortable with her body, or who shows that she is willing to be naughty and take herself less seriously. Most likely, he didn't call back because he didn't feel any of the sexual chemistry he was hoping to find.

He didn't call me back because
he's flaky and doesn't want commitment

Even if a guy has already decided before the first date that he doesn't want anything serious, it doesn't mean he's going to go on a date, then suddenly disappear. Even the most dedicated bachelor enjoys having a dating life. He could go on a dozen dates with someone with whom he's having mind-blowing sex, but still consider himself as someone who doesn't want commitment. Just because he doesn't want commitment doesn't mean he's going to run out after one or two dates. Besides, I can't tell you how many confirmed bachelors I've met over the years who, when they meet the right woman, stumble happily head over heels into commitment.

He didn't call me back because
he was only after sex

In order to understand just how ridiculous this assumption is we need to be clear about two things relating to men. First, no matter what they tell you, most of them are not having regular sex outside a relationship. Second, the guys who are having regular sex are often having it with the same person.

Why is this relevant? Because—and I am sure you don't need me to convince you more about this—men are pretty big on sex. They are so into sex, they don't give it up when there's no reason. Especially sex they enjoy.

I always laugh at the stereotype of the hit-it-and-quit-it guy, who supposedly lies in bed the morning after a night of great sex thinking, Phew, I need to get out of here and never call again so that that doesn't happen again anytime soon.

My point is, a guy who gets sex (especially sex he likes) will call again even if it's just for the sex at the end of a night. Even the biggest player will keep calling for sex. The vast majority of men are not having so much sex offered to them that they can afford not to call back a woman with whom they had an exciting night of passion.

If the sex was good, but perhaps the conversation wasn't, he's still going to assume you're up for a booty call. But even if the sex wasn't good, everything else being equal he's probably going to call again. The great comedian Mel Brooks put it this way: For men, sex is like pizza. Even if it's done bad, it's still good.

The point is that if he's not calling, it's not because of the sex.

The Real Reasons He's Not Calling

Men, simpletons though they may be, are surprisingly articulate when it comes to why they're not interested in pursuing a relationship with a woman. Many of their remarks stem from their own insecurities, but the reality is, the following are the kind of things they're thinking. If confronted, a guy might slip into vague mumbo jumbo, but when he's being up front he's likely to say one of the following:

+ She was just nice (there was no edge, no challenge).

+ She was boring.

+ She was too aggressive.

+ She was too superficial.

+ She came across as too desperate.

+ She was trying too hard to impress.

+ She was too negative.

✦ She's a drama queen and would be a nightmare over the long term.

✦ There wasn't any chemistry.

While these reasons may seem all over the map, in the end it comes down to a few basic areas in which the date didn't pan out the way he'd hoped. Let's look at them in more detail.

Lack of sexual chemistry

A guy can go on a date and enjoy a woman's company but still not feel any real attraction. He might think you're the nicest person he's ever met, but if he doesn't feel that pull of sexual energy from your teasing, flirting, and challenging him, the initial visual chemistry he felt peters out. He likes the looks of you, but something isn't working out.

Even if you have perceived value in his eyes and you've managed to connect, he still needs to experience you as a perceived challenge to feel chemistry and deep attraction. Our tendency when we go on a date is to focus on being agreeable. We try to find common topics of interest or connect on something we are passionate about. Being nice might make you a new friend, but it won't create attraction. Being simply pleasant won't repel a guy, but it won't draw him to you, either.

To create the necessary chemistry it's also necessary to stoke the sexual tension with playfulness, teasing, flirting, and breaking rapport. The guy is on the date with you because he's interested in you. But a guy can easily lose his enthusiasm if he doesn't feel a sexual connection as well as an emotional one. Just being nice won't do it.

Lack of complexity

"She seemed one-dimensional" is something I often hear. This translates as only sexy, only funny, only serious, or only career-minded.

She's sexy, but she seems superficial. She's smart and ambitious, but not playful or fun. She's a huge amount of fun! But not sexy. All of these traits are great, but they're part of a whole package; alone they're not enough.

A multidimensional woman displays several sides of her personality during a date. She shows that she has serious values and is dedicated to her career but is also willing to indulge in fun adventures and silly jokes. She shows she is sexy but also has class and doesn't try to seduce everyone. She has accomplishments but she doesn't show them off; she lets him find them out for himself.

Recently I was having breakfast with a single friend of mine; he was giving me the postmortem on a date he'd been on the night before. He'd been at a nightclub the week before and slept with a girl he met on the dance floor that night.

A few days later he texted her to see if they could see each other again. "Why don't we go to dinner?" she texted in return. He agreed, and they set up a date.

Most people would assume that after that dinner my friend would use the opportunity to get her back into bed, but after having taken her to dinner he decided that he didn't want to see her again. I was surprised.

"She was really boring. She had no strong opinions about anything; she didn't banter with me; she wasn't particularly playful. She doesn't seem to have ambitions, hobbies, or passions. By the end of dinner I barely knew any more about her than when I started. I couldn't imagine going home with her because I don't know what we'd talk about when we weren't having sex!"

If this guy couldn't envisage what they would talk about before and after sex on a single evening, he surely couldn't imagine how they would ever pass the time during the day-to-day events that occur in a committed relationship.

The real tragedy is the misunderstanding this will create. The woman will go back to her friends and wonder why he didn't even try to take her home (even if she was planning to say no) and why he never called her again. After all, he was the one who asked to see her again, he agreed to dinner, and he picked up the check. Why had he suddenly turned into such a jerk?

Her friends are unlikely to know what she's like on a date. They probably won't realize that she bored him senseless. Chances are they'll look at the situation and say something like, "It's probably because you slept with him too soon," which had nothing to do with it.

Because she'll never know the real reason, she'll focus on sleeping with men too soon as the source of her pain, and maybe even form a belief that all men run away after sex, rather than the fact that her personality doesn't come across well in the cold light of day.

She was needy and desperate

Men have a sixth sense for a woman who gives off the vibe of needing to fill a relationship-shaped hole. Worse, if she is oversharing about her plans to get married as soon as possible and have children, she might as well be holding up a sign that says, "Yes, I'm that scary. Please don't call me for another date, ever."

It's not because a guy doesn't want all of these things, it's because he doesn't like feeling as if he's the target in your big plan of bagging an eligible male as soon as possible. Men always need to feel chosen for a unique reason. In the early stages, he wants to feel like you haven't got it all planned out. He wants to feel like anything can happen—and yes, marriage and children might, in the end, be what happens.

This is admittedly extreme. Perhaps you know better than to introduce the topic of whether you should send your future children to public or private school over appetizers, but there are other, less obvious ways of sending the message that you're a little needy.

If there's one bit of wisdom regarding men that all women should embed into their psyches now and forever, it's this: men love *complimenting* women, but hate *reassuring* them.

If a guy compliments you, just smile and thank him. You can even say, "Why, thank you!" in a way that conveys that you're a little bit surprised to hear this, but that's it. This is the only high-value way to respond to a compliment. Accept it graciously.

A never-to-be-broken rule: don't reject his compliment. If he says you look sexy in the morning, don't respond with "God no, I look disgusting like this."

If he says you look hot in that skirt, don't make him repeat it. Neediness rears its unattractive head because we feel grateful that someone is complimenting us, as opposed to accepting that we deserved the compliment. Our insecurity may compel us to ask, "Oh, do you really think so?" in the hopes of wringing more validation out of the compliment. It's awkward and a turnoff, and you never want to seem too grateful that a man is saying something nice to you.

Topics to Avoid on a First Date

When you're a high-value woman, your conversation needs to bear this out. As Benjamin Franklin observed, "Remember not only to say the right thing in the right place, but far more difficult still, to leave *unsaid* the wrong thing at the tempting moment."

But sometimes we don't really know what that wrong thing is, or nerves get the best of us and we blurt out what we're thinking. Many of us repeat the same bad conversational habits during dates for years, without being aware that we're turning off a guy who might otherwise grow to love us.

Never dish about your ex

If you find yourself straying into anecdotes about your ex, swiftly cut yourself off. Even if it's lighthearted or relevant to the situation, the fact that your ex is a viable topic of conversation will spell disaster for any man you're trying to attract.

Never rant about your ex and how much you can't stand him. You may think you're showing it's over with him, but you're doing the exact opposite. Your date will probably assume that you still have hang-ups about your ex, or that you have a load of unresolved emotional baggage that he doesn't want to take on. Worse, it may appear to a guy that you've had a string of bad relationships, and he may start wondering whether the problem wasn't with your exes but with you.

Whenever we complain about an ex, we risk coming across as a victim, which is never sexy or intriguing.

The same reasoning goes for the opposite conversation—a guy doesn't want to hear about how great your last boyfriend was either. Basically, a guy doesn't need to know about any lingering emotional attachments you might have. It's best to keep these to yourself.

Avoid talking about your weight

Not only is your weight a boring topic best reserved for your girlfriends, it's an irrelevant one. He's on a date with you, therefore he finds you appealing. There is not a single scenario that exists on a first date where you should be discussing your insecurities about your figure. Even if something happens that requires him to strip off all your clothes, throw you over his shoulder, and run down Main Street, make no cracks about how heavy you must be, how he's going to need a chiropractor after this, nothing. If you're on a date with him, you're a hot chick. Period.

Some insecure phrases that should never leave your lips on a date, ever again

"Really? Do you REALLY think I'm pretty/skinny/sexy?"

What you're really saying: Please repeat the compliment so I can feel that buzz of acceptance again. I'm insecure and rely on other people's approval to validate my sense of self.

"Oh no, I'm not that sexy/pretty/hot. There are so many beautiful girls in this place."

What you're really saying: I need more reassurance because I'm intimidated by the situation. Keep telling me that I'm pretty so I can get over this inferiority complex.

"Guys never ask me out. I haven't been on a date in ages."

What you're really saying: It's pretty obvious I'm into you, so I want to make it as easy for you as possible, even at the expense of sounding like a castoff. If a guy ever asks you why you're still single, make it about your standards. Tell him, "If I'm going to be with someone, he has to be really great. I'm not someone who just falls into relationships."

Insecurity can bring any relationship to its knees, particularly if one partner is much more secure than the other. So many times I hear from men who are torn up about having to leave their girlfriends over this issue. When I ask the guy why he left, so many times he answers, "She's a great girl, but I just felt drained by her. She's so insecure. She always got jealous when I'd speak to other girls, or needed me to keep assuring her I'm not attracted to anyone else but her."

Needing constant validation from someone else indicates that we don't have internal certainty. True certainty means never having to look to anyone else to remind ourselves that we are desirable.

What If Seeing Him Only Ever Happens on His Terms?

Sometimes the problem isn't that a guy doesn't call, but that he only calls when it's convenient for him. He's still in contact with you, but there's no doubt that he's squeezing you into his schedule, rather than making you even a midlevel priority in his life.

Full disclosure: I've been known to be that guy.

Not long ago I'd been seeing a woman for several months. The problem, of course, was that we weren't actually seeing each other at all. I was working seven days a week growing my business. Half the time, I was running Get the Guy seminars in various foreign cities, so I wasn't even in the country.

She would ask me when I was available, attempt to arrange something, and then at the last minute I would have to cancel. When I would try to arrange something, it would always be at the last possible moment when I knew I was free, and even then my invitation would be for something convenient like meeting for a drink before I dashed off to the airport.

Too many women do things on a guy's terms, and when they do, rather than seeming cool and accommodating, they lose his respect. This particular woman wasn't having any of it. She gave me a reality check when, after yet another last-minute flurry of frantic plan making, where I tried to squeeze her in for an hour between meetings, she sent me this text: "I'm not really a one-hour time slot kind of girl, call me when you have some proper time to spend :-) xo."

This was a great high-value message. It immediately elevated her in my esteem. I got the message loud and clear that she was not a woman to call only when it was easy for me or when I could fit her in. I liked this woman, and had no bad intentions with regard to her, but this was a huge wake-up call: If I wanted to pursue her, I needed to give her the time and attention she deserved.

What I loved about her response was that she managed to be playful and unemotional while implying, "The door is open for when you want to do better." Isn't that brilliant?

16

Premature Obligation

You've found a guy.

You've had two coffee dates and spent a day at an amusement park. Or, you went to a music festival and spent an afternoon catching up on work and eating takeout. You like him and he likes you.

Maybe he's Mr. Perfect, or maybe he's just enough to get excited about, or maybe he's just better than no one. The fact is, just thinking about him makes your heart race. There seems to be a man in your life. Your thoughts run wild. You can't resist picturing what your next meeting will be like. Quickly, your thoughts mutate into vacationing together, and what you're going to buy him for his birthday, and inviting him home for Thanksgiving, and before you know it you're wondering if he could be *the* guy.

Suddenly you find yourself trying to get more time with him. Suddenly you're canceling activities to free up your schedule. Suddenly you have no interest in going out to meet anyone else. Now all your focus is on him. Now you arrange your life around being there for him. You wonder what you can do to nudge your budding relationship along more quickly. You try to steer conversations toward talk of "what" the two of you are, since you want to move toward exclusivity as soon as possible.

While all of this is going on inside your head, he's still mulling over what restaurant to take you to for your next date.

The problem is this: the moment you start focusing on the future while he's still thinking of where you're going to eat tonight, he begins to wonder how the two of you are so out of sync. Ironically, even if he was considering moving toward something more meaningful, his reaction is to back away. Why?

The first reason is that he hasn't had time to sell himself on the idea of the two of you as a couple yet. He needs space to do this.

The second reason is that he begins to see you as low value, which makes the first reason even more difficult for him. All of the hard work you've done to be of perceived value and challenge flies out the window in service of pleasing him. Don't make this mistake.

Why does this happen? It's not because women aren't picky. Most women are incredibly articulate about exactly what they want in a man. Why is it then that so many women seem to want to establish a relationship with guys they don't really even know?

The Folly of Making Mr. Right

It's not uncommon for a woman to want a relationship so badly that she finds a way to mold *any* guy into the image of the *right* guy. She takes a guy with one or two qualities she likes and fills in the blanks, imbuing him with the rest of the qualities she requires. She turns him into Prince Charming (which is usually far from the truth) and winds up valuing him too highly. This creates a false reality, since the guy hasn't earned the image she has of him. He may be a great guy but for reasons entirely different than her notion of him.

Even women who are good about *not* imbuing a guy with qualities he doesn't possess can fall into the trap of confusing the traits he manifests in other areas of life with what he's bringing to her.

Often when a woman comes across a seemingly successful, charming, and articulate man, she starts ticking off the criteria she has for Mr. Right. The more she watches him move through the world, the more she sees him interacting successfully with other people and watches how he conducts his business or the way he works a room, the more she risks thinking, Wow, this guy is so great. He really does possess everything I want in a guy. Now I want to go and communicate how much I like him.

What's wrong with this? She's allowing herself to fall for someone who may be a wonder of the world in his own life but who has done nothing special in relation to her. He might be a great human being, but that doesn't necessarily make him a great catch. What makes a guy a great catch is how he relates to you. He may have earned your approval as a person, but he hasn't earned your approval as a partner until he really invests in you.

I can't say this enough: a guy must be evaluated based only on what he does for *you*.

The Object of Your Affection

It strikes me that guys get a bad rap when it comes to objectifying women. There's no doubt that they do it. You'd be hard-pressed to find a guy who hasn't looked at an attractive woman some time in his postpubescent life and thought, I'd tap that.

But I would venture to say that women also objectify men. When they rate a man based on his success, his status, his power, his general allure, without knowing him or having any sort of a relationship with him, are they not doing the same thing? We all have a tendency to objectify people without knowing or being close them. When we do this it prevents us from having a real relationship with someone, because we are not relating to them but to a set of characteristics that have no bearing on personal connection.

Any of these attitudes can lead a woman to obligate herself prematurely to someone who doesn't yet deserve her focus. She in turn expects reciprocated obligation before it's warranted. This is often a result of the female propensity to select the *most desirable* male, which is in direct conflict with a man's tendency to select the *next* female. The following may be a broad generalization, but it makes the point rather neatly:

Give a man ten women and he'll play.

Give a woman ten men and she'll choose.

This doesn't mean men don't want to settle down, but their instinct is to explore their options. A woman's instinct is to quickly discard men she doesn't like and settle on the one guy she likes the most. The rest she then ignores. Does this mean she has to become more like a man and play around? Not at all. My point is that rather than concentrate on perhaps forcing a relationship with a single guy she still needs to get to know better, she needs to spend more time with more guys before she narrows her focus. By the way, when a woman does move slower, the guy's inclination will be to move faster. He'll wonder why she's just going with the flow and not pushing him toward commitment. The perceived challenge increases as he wonders what he needs to do to make her want only him. Her perceived value increases as he sees that she's more discerning than to just rush into commitment with someone who hasn't really gone out of his way for her yet. He now begins to work for her. As we know, everyone values what they work for, and this valuing continues once they get what they want.

How to Know When He's Become Worth It

Suppose you held a bank account into which the guy is depositing money, and you couldn't move into a serious situation with him until he deposited a certain amount. How does he build up this credit with you?

He thinks of you in his actions: he makes an effort to see you, he shows generosity and selflessness, and he looks out for your best interests. He supports you. In short, he works to earn you. When he's built up that credit in the bank, you may reward him, and when you do, he'll associate that reward with having invested in you. He now learns that the best way to be rewarded by you is to invest more.

Compare this with the situation above. She decides she likes him based on what she sees in him—she essentially gives him unlimited credit—and tries to pin him down. He has no credit in the bank because he hasn't actually done anything specifically for her. So when she tries to force the commitment, he associates it with having done nothing to earn her.

Remember: men don't value what they didn't earn in the first place.

A guy's value should be based only on how he treats you.

Contrary to so many romantic movies, it's never enough that a guy merely likes you, or even loves you. Plenty of men love women they treat like crap. Your decision to choose him should be based on what he does in relation to you and how he communicates his feelings, not just on how he feels.

A guy worth considering for a serious relationship cherishes you, and if he cherishes you, he shows it. He must display these behaviors before you decide to choose him. Anyone else isn't the guy for you.

PART THREE

Keep the Guy

17

═══

How to Be the Woman of His Dreams

I cringe whenever I receive e-mails from women who say, "Hey Matt, I've loved following your advice for the last six months but I'm unsubscribing to your e-mails now. I've found a boyfriend. Thanks for everything!"

While I am always appreciative of the expressed gratitude, I always feel like the sender has missed the point. To see getting into a relationship as the endgame is to have bought into the old Hollywood ending. The couple finally gets together; they kiss; they marry; the romantic music swells to a crescendo; the credits roll. And they live happily ever after.

In real life, nothing of the sort happens. Your relationship, if it is to last, needs tending to keep growing. You've got the guy, now you need to figure out whether you want to keep him. If you do decide you want a lasting relationship, how do you increase the possibility that it will continue in a fulfilling way?

Many of the principles that we have learned up to this point are still relevant when it comes to nurturing and building a relationship for long-lasting love. When you believe you are with The One, it is not a time to sit back and become complacent. All that is good in your life needs continuous nurturing: your body, your profession, your friendships, your familial connections, and yes, your love life. In this case, the nurturing flows in both directions. You need to be sure you are getting what you need from him, and he needs to feel that what he is getting from you could come from no other.

The Five Things That Make a Guy Wild for His Woman

In this next section, I am going to reveal a guy's deepest needs. It may seem like the work is one-sided. But remember, in my coaching of guys, I give them plenty of work to do as well. So bear with me on this. A careful read will help you understand the very simple but atavistic triggers you can tap in a man's psyche to become the woman he will want forever.

He needs sexual validation

We've seen in chapter 13 the degree to which a guy's self-esteem is linked to the validation he receives from sex. Whether you're on your tenth date or in your tenth year of the relationship, a guy never ever outgrows his need to feel worthy sexually. This isn't *just* about the two of you having sex, but about him feeling like he's able to turn you on.

His sense of worth as a man is inextricably linked to how much you desire him sexually. He needs to feel as though he's everything you ever needed in that arena. While he may be able to acknowledge that there are men more physically attractive than he, guys with six-pack abs or with more striking eyes, he needs to know that you derive complete sexual satisfaction from him. No matter how emotionally close a guy feels to you, he will always possess that crucial need. And this becomes even more important in a relationship.

Of course women also want to have a passionate, fulfilling sex life, and they need to feel sexually desired. These needs aren't gender specific. But it's important to grasp the profound degree to which feeling masculine is intricately linked to a guy's ability to turn you on. You have a frightening power at your disposal, because this never stops being important to us. If he feels sexually unworthy, he feels unworthy as a man, which he grows to resent.

One of the big mistakes women sometimes make is failing to show the same sexual validation they displayed in the early stages of the relationship. They stop telling him how sexy he looks, or how much they love his body, or how attracted they are to him. He needs to see that he keeps turning you on, over time. Our culture often paints a picture of a woman's need to be physically validated, but the truth is, men are often more needy than women are in this arena. When you show him you're interested in him sexually, you're also informing his behavior and *making him more the kind of man you want him to be.*

Fortunately, sexually validating your guy isn't difficult. It's actually easy—perhaps too easy. Alarmingly easy. The technique I'm about to tell you about is powerful beyond measure. You must take a solemn vow never to use it for evil.

I wrestled with whether to include what follows. Women have no idea how much power resides in the words they use. If you want to start affecting his behavior this very minute, consider what you say. Men are completely powerless in the face of phrases like:

"I can't resist it when you . . ."

"It really turns me on when you . . ."

"God, you are so sexy when you . . ."

For example, if you want him to satisfy you sexually, you have to tell him when he's getting it right. Tell him, "It really turns me on when you do that." Or "I can't resist you when you . . ." If something he does pleases you in bed, for God's sake, moan louder! Make sure he registers that he's pleasing you. You must believe me: if a man hears that something he does turns you on, he will never, ever forget it. A guy cherishes moments like these and holds them in his heart forever. If you simply tell him, "I can't resist you in that shirt" or "It really turns me on when you kiss me that way," expect to see that shirt a lot and always be kissed that way.

The genius of this is that you get to tell your guy exactly what you like, and he'll *want* to do it as often as possible. And the biggest secret of all is that this technique works even when your comments are un-related to sex. If you tell a guy that his strong biceps really turn you on, he'll do fifty pull-ups before you come over next time. This is not an exaggeration. If you say, "It really turns me on when you surprise me," you can expect to be surprised more often than you may like! I remember a friend being told by his girlfriend that she was really turned on by the idea of him buying her underwear, and suddenly that was the only thing he could think of to buy for her birthday and Christmas presents.

I'm genuinely reluctant to be giving this knowledge away. I have a recurring nightmare where I see tribes of men washing your cars, pol-ishing your apartment floors, cleaning your shoes, all because you've told them how much seeing them do those things turns you on.

He needs someone who recognizes his uniqueness

Every man is looking for the woman who sees him as different from every other man in the world. He wants to feel that there are spe-cial things about him that you admire, that no other man can give you. He needs to feel that he has been chosen for a specific reason. The powerful corollary here is that a man will not want to lose the woman who knows him and appreciates him in way that is essential to the way he sees himself. If he does lose that woman, he doesn't only lose her, he loses the way she sees him and how he likes to see himself.

A man who is accomplished wants to be adored for the traits that got him there, as opposed to the external results of his hard work. Plenty of people are attracted to his money, status, and power, so being admired for those things doesn't make him feel special. The woman who isn't unduly impressed by his achievements but who understands the strength of his character is the one he desires. He needs to feel that if he lost everything, the woman he's with would still choose him over every other man on earth.

When you praise your boyfriend or partner, be as specific as possible. I remember being on the phone with a girlfriend once when I was standing by a lake. I told her how from where I was standing I could see some baby ducks paddling around and that I wished she could see how cute they were, to which she said, "I love that about you, Matt. You're this strong masculine guy but you also have this really sweet gentle side that comes out now and then." I was immensely flattered. If she had just said, "Aww, you're sweet," it wouldn't have had the same impact because it sounds like a generic response. Because she made it specific about something in my personality she admired, it became a compliment that I never forgot.

Men are more sentimental about this than women realize. If he feels that you have never met a man like him, he feels special around you on a level you can't imagine.

And because he feels special around you, *you become special to him.*

There's a scene in *Casino Royale* in which, after James Bond is recovering from having been beaten up, tortured, and nearly killed, Vesper Lynd confesses her admiration for his bravery by saying, "If the only thing left of you was your smile and your little finger, you'd still be more of a man than anyone I've ever known."

This kind of admiration is important, because it makes a guy feel as if you get him on a level that no one else could. I'm not advising you to go in for senseless flattery or ego stroking. Your admiration has to be genuine. This is about connecting with your partner and showing him that you truly understand him. That genuine connection puts you in a category above anyone else in his life.

He needs a loyal teammate

The best couples are a team, two people who are on each other's side and want the best for one another. Often we hear the word "loyalty" and assume it means sexual fidelity, but this consistent, reliable having-the-other's-back behavior encompasses a loyalty deeper than monogamy alone.

It goes without saying that this quality needs to be reciprocated equally by both sides. Loyalty is about supporting the other person's goals, unselfishly. It's about willing him to succeed, living in the enjoyment of his fulfilling his dreams, even when some of those dreams may be personal. The mindset behind this kind of loyalty is simple: if it affects one of us, it affects both of us.

Be loyal to him when you're with his friends. Be loyal to him in anyone else's company, for that matter. Men are perhaps more sensitive than women about this. If you put him down in other people's company, don't back him up in public, or show doubt in his ability to do something, it sends an unmistakable message that says, "I don't really value you as a man."

He wants someone who will stand by him. Take care not to jump on a bandwagon when people are making jokes at his expense. His pals can get away with it, but be wary of joining in. He needs his partner to resist and to root for him, even when it's only a matter of playfully coming to his defense. When you show in that moment that you're on his side, it makes him appreciate you even more.

To be a loyal partner doesn't require that you agree with him, but it does require you to make an effort to see his point of view and refuse to do anything that might undermine his confidence.

The most successful couples enhance each other's lives and help each other to be better. They don't compete or get in each other's way. As a team, you feel that you are better together than you might be apart.

He needs to protect and provide

The masculine nature needs to provide and protect. This includes the need to protect himself as well as others. Men are generally taught from an early age to protect themselves against emotional vulnerability; in the event they have to go out into the world and conquer fearsome things, they need to be able to focus on the task at hand. There's no place for emotion in this; indeed, being in the thrall of deep feelings may prevent them from protecting and providing.

When a boy cries, he's often told to stop crying. He's told that he has to hold it together, to be strong. At school, he's taught not to show his feelings in front of other males. If a guy gets upset in school, he doesn't look to other guys to take care of him. He's taught instead to hide it. Thus, guys make their way through the world holding in their emotions, not expressing them. I am not judging whether this is the most emotionally progressive or healthy way to live, but the fact remains that these are the tenets of male development and nurturing. It pays to heed the facts. Most important, men feel most themselves when they're containing their feelings in the service of protecting and providing.

In the wake of modern feminism this idea might seem outdated, and in the traditional sense it might be. Generations ago men fulfilled their need to protect and provide by making the money. Indeed, that's all a lot of them did. But in the twenty-first century, women make significant or greater contributions to household finances, so guys do have to step up their game. Simply bringing home a paycheck, slapping it on the counter, then popping open a beer and sitting on the couch won't cut it anymore. (Frightening that it ever did, but that's for another book.)

A man needs to feel he's providing *something* for you. He needs to feel on some level that he serves a purpose in your life and is giving you something you couldn't get from anyone else.

Being a strong and independent girlfriend or wife is not what emasculates a man. Indeed, your being independent is part of what makes you a high-value woman. It's part of why he's attracted to you. But if he hears you say something like "I don't need a man for anything. I can do it all myself," he naturally wonders what's the point of being in a relationship with you. If you have no needs and require nothing of him, then he questions his purpose.

A man feels emasculated when he feels like he's dispensable in your life and that you could happily go on without him. He needs to be your man who can be there for you.

I was reminded of how difficult the situation can be for both men and women while watching an old Woody Allen film, *Hannah and Her Sisters.* Elliot and Hannah are arguing about how little he feels she needs him. He says, "I need someone I can matter to. It's hard to be around someone who gives so much and needs so little in return." She replies that she does have needs, but he says, frustrated, "Well, I can't see them!"

Hannah is a wealthy, successful actress and works hard to always make sure everyone is happy. She gives so much to everyone around her, but her husband, Elliot, is lost in the relationship. He doesn't feel he has any place. He needs someone to whom he matters. The tragedy is that Hannah does indeed have needs, but they're invisible to Elliot. She never shows any need; she never shows her husband what she gets from him. And because of this lack of communication, he feels useless in the relationship.

There is no contradiction between being a strong woman and needing a man. I don't want you to confuse this with neediness, which is a form of desperation. When you're in a relationship, your guy needs to feel needed.

Even if you're not the breadwinner, chances are you also work.

Allowing him to help shore you up after a bad day is a form of allowing him to protect and provide. When you've had a bad day, share it with him. You may think you're saving him from the boring details of the office by saying, "I just had a bad day, don't worry," but the effect is to shut him out, preventing him from saying something that might help.

Another way of communicating your need for his help is by simply letting him know you've had a lousy day. Saying, "Work really sucked today. I really need to just be close to you tonight and cuddle," permits him to be there for you. It allows him to feel as if he's the only one who could comfort you.

No matter how far along we have come to closing the gender gap economically, socially, and culturally, deep down inside he feels he needs to take care of you. If you don't find some way of making him feel like you need him, his sense of self-worth begins to erode.

The good news is that letting your guy know how important he is to you isn't difficult or demanding. A kiss and a hug while saying "I missed you so much today" or "I wanted to get home to you so badly" works wonders.

He needs to be nurtured and supported

When a guy enters a relationship he needs to feel as if his partner is the best supporter he's ever had. He needs to feel like you are cheering him on, supporting his ambition, being completely behind him.

What's the greatest way to nurture a guy? *Believe in him.* If you believe in him, a guy is going to want to be around you for a long time. A woman who believes in our vision, what we're capable of, and who we are as a man is someone who gives us strength that no one else can. We want to hold on to that. If you tell him, "If anyone can do it, you can," you are the most special thing to him in the world.

We all have self-doubt sometimes, but when he has those moments and you show him that you completely believe in his potential, he'll strive so much harder because of that support. Seeing him as able to be better than he is creates a positive feedback loop. You will get the best of him when you bolster him.

This does *not* mean you are living for his potential. You're happy with him now; he already meets your standards. But he needs to see that you believe in his ability to get what he wants and fulfill the potential that he sees for himself. It's giving him something to aspire to. The worst thing for a guy is feeling that he has this big project but that his partner either (a) doesn't back him or (b) doesn't even pay attention to it. He wants you to be interested and support the things he cares about. He wants you to be excited about the vision he's excited about for himself.

===

I realize that advising you to show a man you need him, to nurture and support him, and to allow him to protect and provide for you may seem to fly in the face of everything that's come before. You may be wondering how can it be that as a high-value woman you're both certain and independent, and not reliant on a man to be fulfilled, yet also need to show your man that you need him. The primary difference is that now we're talking about keeping the guy, about the necessity of showing vulnerability in order to connect and share love. All of us, even the most centered, strong-willed, and positive among us, have moments when we feel vulnerable or have needs that run so deep, we barely know that they are there. The beauty of a committed relationship is that it allows you to share those feelings and by doing so, strengthen the bonds you have with one another.

Every man in the world is looking for the woman who needs him but isn't dependent upon him; who is sexual but is more than just a seductress; who is kind and generous but not validation seeking; who is loyal and supports his growth but doesn't tell him how to live; who fights for her man but is not jealous; who is independent but makes him feel like the most important person in her life; who kicks ass out there in the world but lets herself be vulnerable and gentle with him.

This may seem like asking for a lot, but it all circles back to you as the woman of high value you already are. Only now you are creating a lasting bond by digging deeper to connect the male psyche with the very qualities you embody.

18

===

Is He Mr. Right?

Now that you have him and you have become the woman of his dreams, how do you know if this guy is right for you? If it's six days, six months, or six years down the line, how do you know he's worth your continued time, effort, and love?

In earlier chapters I discussed the importance of setting standards and of not wasting a single moment on a guy who didn't meet them. This ritual alone will help weed out the guys who are wrong for you, probably within the first two weeks of knowing them. One of the toughest things to do during the getting the guy and keeping the guy stages is to refuse to get wrapped up in a romance unless the guy genuinely deserves it. Sometimes, we want to be in a relationship so badly that we settle, even in the very early stages.

We ignore obvious problems because we want to be swept off our feet. But inevitably, these difficulties come back to haunt us. When a long-term relationship ends, if we search our hearts and are honest with ourselves, we may realize that we ignored the warning signs because we were hoping against hope that we'd found our soul mate. Remember that people are always showing you who they are.

A woman friend told me not long ago about her breakup. After two years, she broke up with her boyfriend because he was constantly going out and getting drunk with his buddies. When she was telling me the story, she spoke in a way that suggested she never saw it coming.

I asked her what they did on their first few dates, and she told me that they'd had a great time going out and getting drunk. When I suggested the connection between her early dates with the guy and his current behavior, she was floored. Sometimes the signs are subtle, but we must learn to read and evaluate them. If something bothers us early on, we need to heed our instincts or risk finding ourselves far down the road with someone who doesn't deserve our love, support, attention, and fidelity. A wise friend once said, "A relationship often ends the same way that it begins."

How to Know If He's for You

We can never be 100 percent sure how any relationship will turn out. Part of what makes us delirious about love is that mystery. You don't know what will happen. Of course, that is true in all of life. However, we've spent time building up a knowledge base to put you in a position to find and keep a great love of your life. Now we get to put some of that to use by asking some hard questions about whether he is worthy of your delirious love. Here is what you need to be certain about.

He prioritizes the values you also think are important

What is most important to *you* in life? Is it a sense of adventure? Is it ambition? Is it kindness? Family? Generosity? Security?

It's vital to find someone who not only shares your values but also ranks them in a similar order of importance.

Let's say you meet a nice guy and during the first few weeks of your dating life you tell him that family is important to you. You say your family means a lot to you, and he agrees, and it seems as if you share something important. It's wonderful! You don't press him on the matter, and all is well until you've been dating for a few months and you want him to come to Sunday night dinner at your parents' house, but he doesn't want to. He sees his own family only on the holidays. Now there's conflict. He doesn't understand why you need so much family togetherness, and you think that either he misled you, he doesn't care about family, or he just doesn't like your family. He might well care, but just not as much as you do. This difference in priority was never forced into the light during your courtship.

If his priority list of values puts, say, career, adventure, and intimacy before family, he's always going to put work, travel, and being with you above being closer to your family. Meanwhile, on your list, family might be number one and career number four. If this is the case, every time the issue of spending time with family arises, there's likely to be a conflict.

Often while we're getting to know someone we find ourselves attracted to one value they manifest, without stopping to consider others that are equally important to us. We might be so blinded by that one quality that we even go so far as to imagine that this person has others we've yet to see displayed. A woman might fall for a man because he values ambition, and she finds that sexy, but later, as she gets to know him better, she realizes that he doesn't value connection and intimacy nearly as much as she would like. The result is that his ambition keeps him working all the time, while his relatively low ranking of connection on his own list of values contributes to her feeling unloved and neglected.

You may be thinking, but what about the theory that opposites attract? We've all known couples where she was outgoing and he was reserved, or he was gregarious and she was quiet. These are personality traits, not values. Despite their different styles, both people need to value the same things to more or less the same degree.

It's not just his values, it's his standards

This one takes some explaining.

Think of it this way: for every one of your values, be it adventure, intelligence, or generosity, you have a standard for how intensely you pursue that value.

Two people could both value adventure, but this doesn't mean they both have the same standards when it comes to being adventurous. One person's idea of adventure might be climbing Mount Kilimanjaro, while their partner's is trying a new restaurant. They share the same core value, but their standard for adventure is different.

To make things more complicated, someone can claim that a value is important to him but not necessarily live by it.

Let me give you a scenario: A man regularly insults his wife. Her friends and family can't understand why she takes it, why she doesn't just leave. How could she stay with someone who treats her with such disrespect? But what we miss is that every once in a while he does something incredibly sweet and kind—he kisses her affectionately, apologizes profusely, commits an act of generosity meant to tilt the balance for the good. In those moments he will claim that the unkind person is not who he really is, that underneath it all he is just a man who loves her and never wants to hurt her. It is some inner demon, he claims, that causes him to behave badly. Let's be clear, he may fully mean these words when he says them. However, what matters is the average of his actions, not the average of his words.

The woman in this example will see the small glimpses of kindness—a value that she happens to rate highly—and use them to convince herself that he is indeed the man she wants, despite his abuse. So she stays, in the hope that she can bring this sweet and loving man out more so that the abuse will stop. If she is good enough, he will treat her well always.

Though it sounds crazy, he and she can actually have the same value of kindness. But one of them is living this value on a daily basis and the other one is not. It's like when someone says, "I'm a really loving person," but you never really see evidence of it. What they are really saying is that "being loving" is a value they aspire to, but that's not the same as living it.

Have you ever dated a guy who talks about how ambitious he is and all of his dreams but never steps outside his comfort zone, or never actually puts in the effort to work for what he claims he wants? He may blame his lack of success on external factors, never fully taking responsibility for his stasis. He may well wish he had ambition and was working on his dream, but that is not the same as actually living it.

Here's why this concept is so relevant to our happiness moving forward: even if you've discussed your core values with a guy, and he agreed with you when it came to those that were most important, unless you see him demonstrating his values in the way he lives, it doesn't matter that he gives them lip service. Our relationship choices must be based on the man's current standards. Fall in love with the man in front of you, not his potential.

Does that mean that people don't grow or change? Of course not. I do what I do because I believe in the power of people to change. But I also know it's foolish to predict how much our influence will promote change in someone and even more foolish to stake our future happiness on it.

When we meet someone, from our very first conversation, we need to be observant. Is the person to whom we're attracted demonstrating through their actions that they share our values? Over the course of spending real time together, do we witness them exhibiting the same standards for these values as we hold in our own life?

I'm not suggesting his actions need to match your own. We don't have to live these values in the same way. Living the value of generosity for one person may express itself in how he treats family and friends; for another person it might be the charity work he does every week. How each person lives his or her values is not as important as both being committed to them at the same depth.

If a guy says he'll change, how do you know if he means it?

There are two values that I believe to be vital to a relationship. If you both possess and display these two values, the potential exists to work through your differences.

The two values are *growth* and *teamwork*.

If you value personal growth and your guy doesn't, the chances of him changing are extremely low. He may alter his behavior initially for fear of losing you, but long-term change requires determination and commitment and his belief in the value of growth, regardless of the status of his love life. If your man has no interest in growing for his own sake, he will have no interest in becoming a better man for you.

The second value, teamwork, is just as important. It's the value that makes him want to share in his efforts to make your relationship better and you happier. Teamwork is about his belief that the two of you, working together, can fix whatever dynamics in the relationship aren't working.

Again, if you want to know whether a man values these things, watch his actions. When you tell him what would make you happier, does he listen and strive to follow through on it? Or does he become defensive and deflect your needs in service to his ego? When you are in need, does he look for ways to help you, or does he retreat?

It's less important that he figures out the exact ways to make you happy than that he's making a concerted effort. Because you are a team, you can guide him along the way. What's important is that he possesses the underlying value that makes him want to make you happy. You can work with him on steering his approach—this is the work of being in a relationship—but you can't create the intention behind it.

One word of caution: the shared values of growth and teamwork are most likely to contribute to a successful relationship when the other values the two of you share, and your standards for them, are similar. If you meet a guy with wildly different values, no amount of "trying" is likely to mold him into the man you want him to be.

What to Do When You Need to Forget the Guy

I've shown you how to find, choose, and attract a guy, and how then to work at developing and maintaining the right relationship with him. I've explained how men's minds work, to better help you achieve a better outcome in love. I suggested ways of thinking and behaving that will also enrich your life and attract men to you.

Nevertheless, sometimes it just doesn't work out.

No matter how well you absorb and apply these principles, no matter how high value you are, how good you are at conveying your value to guys, how faithful you are in applying the rule of reciprocity, or how well you make sure you and your guy share the same values and priorities, you will never be immune to heartbreak. I hope I've taught you how to rig the game in your favor, but it's important to accept that in love, there are still no guarantees. This uncertainty is part of the human condition, part of the mystery of love.

You may do absolutely everything right and still get hurt or be disappointed.

We have no control if our partner decides to up and leave. We have no control if our partner decides to be unfaithful. Sometimes you will be the one who falls out of love or who realizes that this person just isn't right for you. Most of us understand that all we can control is our own actions; we can only influence the actions and behaviors of someone else. Then there's our own unruly heart, causing trouble. As so many of you know all too well, just because you're the one to end it, that doesn't mean your heart isn't broken.

Once in a while I'll have a conversation with a woman about the agony of breakups and she'll say, "I just never really get affected by breakups. I move on straight away. I can't get hurt by guys." I always suspect she's trying to convince herself she doesn't get hurt. It may also mean that she's so afraid of getting burned by love, she refuses to put herself in a situation where she can truly experience that feeling of surrender that's part of falling in love. It's one tactic, certainly, but isn't it better to risk hurt than to allow fear to rule your love life?

If we want the chance to feel the joy of love, we are going to risk feeling more pain than we've ever felt before. When a relationship ends, the pain we experience can take months, even years, to become bearable. Feeling such pain at the loss of a partner is a natural, perhaps even a good, thing; it reassures us that the relationship was meaningful and that we're able to commit to another person at the deepest level. The truth is, we are never ready to be hurt, but that doesn't mean we shouldn't take the risk. First you do the thing you're scared of, and then you get the courage.

How to Move on from Heartbreak

It's over. He took back his toothbrush, T-shirts, and books. You're no longer friends on Facebook. You've deleted his number from your phone. You've instructed your friends to treat him like Voldemort, He-Who-Must-Not-Be-Named.

What matters most at the moment of heartbreak is the meaning we ascribe to our pain. We may feel devastated because we believe we've just lost our soul mate. And that's often what we *do* feel in that moment. When we are deep in heartbreak we feel like we have lost the only person in the world for whom we are capable of feeling this level of emotion. We can't imagine ever loving anyone else.

If we invest in this belief, not only will it increase our suffering, it will also make it more difficult for anyone else to come into our life, because we feel like we've already lost The One. Nothing else seems to matter. We lose our drive, our ambition, and our ability to take even baby steps forward.

But there's another way to look at it.

Consider this: the pain doesn't come from losing your soul mate, but from the disappointment that this guy *wasn't* your soul mate. It's sad, but it's not catastrophic. And if you look at it this way—that in some regard, he failed to live up to your values and standards, so how *could* he have been your soul mate?—the pain is likely to be less severe. I don't mean to minimize the amount it hurts. I've been there, believe me. But by grieving only for your disappointment and dashed expectations, you allow yourself to remain open to the next guy who comes along. It's a much more manageable type of pain. We can now say more easily, "Although I'm hurt right now, this person wasn't right for me. Now I can allow myself to find the right person."

This might sound like a small difference, but just allowing ourselves to take on this more correct understanding of what has happened can free us to move forward. And remember, none of our efforts will have been in vain. We are always learning more about ourselves and our relationships with others. Every experience adds richness to our character, which in turn informs the depth of connection we can make going forward.

NEVER LOOK BACK

I'm going to tell you how to get over any guy once and for all.

Go to **www.gettheguybook.com/getoverhim**
Access code: **gtgbook**

19

What Guys Really Think About the C-Word

Guys aren't born scared of commitment. There's not a gene on the Y chromosome that makes a guy prefer his crappy apartment and video games to a relationship with you.

Usually, somewhere along the way a guy has a bad experience with a girl and develops strong negative associations with commitment. If a guy has suffered in love, his first impulse is not to examine the complexities of the relationship. Indeed, he doesn't want to think about it at all. He's had his heart stomped on, and it's far easier to blame Women, or Relationships, than it is to think too deeply about what went wrong. He turns into a committed bachelor out of a desire to keep himself from getting hurt again. You know this guy. He frequently use phrases like "I don't want to be tied down," "I just want to be free and single," "I just want to enjoy myself and have no responsibilities."

These phrases may make women roll their eyes, and justifiably so, but they also reveal something about the pain men sometimes associate with commitment.

The Truth About Men and the Single Life—
Mr. Bachelor

For Mr. Bachelor, the idea of "settling down" conjures up an image of a bored couple sitting at home on a Friday night watching soap operas, or spending all day Saturday doing household chores. Committing to a relationship looks like the end of all the fun. This perception is reinforced because every guy has a friend who used an excuse like this: "Sorry I can't play poker on Saturday, I promised my girlfriend that I would stay home and hang with her." The girlfriend's showing up with the friend to poker night is simply the other side of this dreaded scenario. The thought that "I" means "we" once he's in a relationship is a real obstacle for Mr. Bachelor. He fears his separate life will end forever.

The modern guy is also bombarded with messages that affect the way he views his ideal lifestyle. Think about the kind of guys who are held up as alpha males on television and in movies. To risk using the analogy one time too often, James Bond's defining characteristics are that he is handsome, suave, perfectly built, impeccably dressed, decisive, and always certain of himself. He also happens to be completely irresistible to women. What's more, he gets to seduce a different woman in every single film, and at the end of that film, either he moves on to someone else or she dies. Consider, for another example, *Mad Men*'s Don Draper, a wealthy advertising genius, who enjoys complete authority in his world. Everyone looks up to him, and guess what. Despite being married (in the early seasons), he sleeps with whomever he pleases.

Mr. Bachelor may aspire to the cool, powerful lives of James Bond and Don Draper, but most will settle for being like the guys in *The Hangover*, hanging out with their bros and avoiding as much responsibility as possible. These guys aren't high powered, but at least they're free to mess around and do what they please. And maybe—who knows?—they might get laid along the way.

Conversely, the wives and girlfriends in these shows and films are often portrayed as too serious and fun-killing. Women must be resisted if you want to keep having fun. Their sole aim in life is to shut down the party and get you hitched as soon as possible.

I'm not suggesting that guys have been completely brainwashed by the culture, but they have been powerfully influenced by it. Worse, that influence is reinforced by their buddies, who watch and absorb the same entertainment and feel the same way. Earlier in the book, you read about how tough it is for a guy to leave his friends and walk across the room to say hello to a woman he finds attractive. This is not dissimilar. If a guy pals around with a group of other single guys, chances are he's going to live in a way that supports being single. What guy hasn't heard from his single friends, "Women just want to pin you down" or "As soon as you get married and have kids you can kiss your dreams good-bye." That those dreams are likely fallacies is beside the point. Mr. Bachelor isn't eager to meet your parents or go shopping for engagement rings.

Why he thinks he's not ready for commitment

Mr. Bachelor imagines his twenties as a golden era in which he envisions himself living with no responsibilities. During this decade he travels and has many awesome adventures, including lots of crazy sexual experiences. He dreams of dating lots of different women with no repercussions. It's a period of ultimate freedom, where he can do everything and anything he wants, without answering to anybody.

Sometime after his thirtieth birthday he'll meet the "right girl." (Women are often portrayed as the romantic ones who dream about meeting a great guy to settle down with, but men are exactly the same.) She'll show up on the scene when he's ticked off every item on his wild and crazy single guy's *101 Things to Do Before the Ball and*

Chain list. Then, when he's reached a certain level of financial stability and he feels that he can provide in some essential way, he'll be ready to settle down.

Of course, this is completely unrealistic. Most guys get to their midthirties and realize they haven't done all those things they thought they were going to do in their twenties. They haven't been jet-setting around the world, haven't been sleeping with a new hot babe every other night, and haven't come close to reaching the peak of their career.

Now, even if the guy is fortunate enough to meet the perfect woman, he still doesn't feel ready. He's afraid of commitment, because it means all these mad adventures he's been hoping to have, all of the wild sex with dozens of women, will now never happen. He may even experience panic, thinking, I'm not supposed to meet this woman yet. I'm not ready to settle down.

What single life is like for most guys

Boring. And lonely.

Unless he's a rock star, a guy isn't living a life of threesomes and driving through Italy in a Ferrari with supermodels. He's not traveling the world living on a sailboat, or inventing a product he can sell to a corporation for half a billion dollars.

For most guys, being single means sitting at home getting drunk with friends and watching movies, or going to nightclubs and trying to find the courage to dance with a girl and eventually ask for her phone number, or texting a girl he doesn't care about just to feel good about himself. If he's lucky, he might land himself a one-night stand. (Take it from a guy, we're always having much less sex than women imagine.)

So why do men remain so attached to the single life? While it's true that the monumental influence of culture has led them to romanticize a reality that doesn't exist, most guys, who are neither shut-ins nor extremely shy, have had a few adventures they cherish. They may be few and far between, but there was that day he went skydiving. There was that trip to Vegas. There's always Saturday poker nights.

The first thing a woman does in a relationship is to change things, or so he assumes. Remember, he is taking his cues from pop culture. She comes over to his apartment and there go the neon beer signs, his favorite chair, and his life-size cardboard Darth Vader. There go his Saturday poker night and the nights when he just sits around in his boxers playing video games and eating three-day-old pizza.

It's not that he's having such a great time being single, but that as long as he is single, he has a perceived freedom that he is unwilling to give up. Somewhere in the recesses of his mind he is thinking, What if that fabulous life is about to present itself at any moment? If he commits, the fantasy of that life dies. If he chooses the wrong girl, he gives up his freedom for naught.

Why He Leaves You, Then Marries the Next Woman He Meets

Typically, when a single guy finds himself in a relationship sometime in his late twenties or early thirties before he thinks he's ready, he goes along with his girlfriend's program. He may genuinely love her. He may genuinely have a terrific time with her. She may enrich his life beyond measure. Still, he believes he's just *not ready*.

Time passes. Then more time passes. They argue, because he doesn't want to spend the Christmas holidays with her parents. Or he wants to go camping with his pals instead of to her best friend's baby shower. Eventually, it comes out: she wants more commitment. Maybe she gives him an ultimatum, saying, "Look, where are we going? Are we serious or not? Because if not, then I can't do this anymore." Now he has a choice. Stay with her, or take his chances being single? Faced with an ultimatum, a guy who is inclined toward the single life will always choose it over the risk of being "trapped" in a relationship, where he believes he'll have too many serious responsibilities, and where it will mean the end of his (imaginary) adventures and autonomy.

He breaks up with his girlfriend or, more likely, he behaves so badly, she's forced to break up with him. Now, he's single again. Hooray! But after a few months of the usual routine, sitting around his apartment drinking with his pals and watching movies, going out to clubs and standing around, it dawns on him that this thing he thought he wanted—freedom!—isn't all it was cracked up to be.

Once he's truly absorbed the truth, he's susceptible to tumbling back into a relationship with the first woman he dates. Maybe he even marries her.

You know what happens next. The first girlfriend, the one he had to leave because he didn't want to commit, gets wind of this and thinks, What the fuck? He told me he didn't want to commit! What she fails to realize is that a guy's ability to delude himself about the glories of being single is immense, and until he gets a reality check or two, he's unlikely to give it up, even for a relationship with someone wonderful. It's the rare man who doesn't reach middle age and feel a tinge of regret about the one who got away.

Enter Mr. Relationship

Of course, many young guys enter committed relationships and get married all the time. They marry their college sweethearts at age twenty-four and are parents by twenty-six. They meet a girl on holiday at twenty-eight and boom, six months later, they're married. Even though Mr. Relationship might miss and even grieve his single life, he understands without a doubt that his perfect woman makes his life much better than it was before.

Mr. Relationship loves sexual variety, adventure, and excitement as much as Mr. Bachelor does, but Mr. Relationship associates these aspects of life with being in a relationship. To Mr. Relationship, having a steady girlfriend, fiancée, or wife means having fantastic sex, since having a committed partner means having regular sex with someone who knows his every quirk and turn-on. He views the woman in his life as someone with whom he can share amazing adventures and experiences. They can backpack through Thailand, go on safari in Kenya, or spend a few weeks together in Paris. With her he experiences companionship and the joy of going through life with someone who understands him at the deepest level. To him, relationships are the ultimate pleasure.

What's more, unlike Mr. Bachelor, Mr. Relationship usually has no illusions about the single life. To him, the single life equals boredom, loneliness, and awkward one-night stands with the occasional girl who doesn't really know what turns him on sexually.

To sum it up, for Mr. Bachelor being single equals sexual satisfaction, adventure, and excitement, and for Mr. Relationship being in a relationship equals sexual satisfaction, adventure, and excitement. The difference between Mr. Bachelor and Mr. Relationship is not that they have different needs. It's not as if Mr. Bachelor *needs* more sexual partners than Mr. Relationship, or that Mr. Relationship needs more intimacy and connection than Mr. Bachelor. It's not that one guy needs a more adventurous lifestyle while another craves a more domestic lifestyle. The only difference between Mr. Bachelor and Mr. Relationship is the *emotions* they associate with commitment.

The Good News

There's an old Jesuit maxim, "Give me a child until he is seven and I will give you the man." For our purposes this means that if you fall in love with a cool twenty-seven-year-old software designer who loves to work all night, sleep all day, and spend all his money on expensive scotch and Mexican vacations, your odds of changing him into someone who goes to bed at 9 p.m. and tucks every last penny into high-yield CDs is exactly zero.

My point: you can't change someone. I know you know this, but I wanted to be clear about it because even though you can't change a guy's character or personality, you *can* alter his emotional associations. You cannot change his basic male needs or desires, but you can change his perception of where those needs can be met within a relationship.

I'm not suggesting you try to logically convince a Mr. Bachelor that a relationship is a good idea. As I said earlier, he associates commitment with the end of everything potentially good in his life, and sitting him down and lecturing him about the benefits of being in a relationship with you only underscores what he already thinks he knows about women: they are first and foremost fun-killers. Even if you were the captain of the debate team and can make the best possible argument for commitment, you still couldn't talk your way into making him think it's a good idea. A guy can't be convinced that he should want a relationship. He has to come to the decision on his own.

But, as we know, actions speak much louder than words. Through your behavior you can show him that being with you is the most fulfilling, varied, adventurous, and sexually satisfying experience he'll ever have, turning your Mr. Bachelor into Mr. Relationship.

FROM CASUAL TO COMMITTED

I talk to a hard-core player who completely changed his mind-set on commitment.

Go to **www.gettheguybook.com/commitment**
Access code: **gtgbook**

20

The Sex Talk (Part II)

There's a moment on the TV show *Curb Your Enthusiasm* that sums up the stereotypical married male's position regarding sex. Larry David is in bed with his wife, who complains, "Why am I always the one who initiates sex?" to which Larry replies, "Just assume that I want it all the time, so whenever you want it, just tap me on the shoulder."

The line is funny because it's completely accurate.

Let's get one thing straight. I know that this isn't always the case. There are some women who find themselves with men whose sex drive is not as active as their own. But what I am addressing in this chapter is how sex relates to the male ego.

The moment your guy decides to be in a committed relationship with you, he has given you permission to be the keeper of his masculinity. I suspect most women don't realize how much trust this involves on the guy's part. He's tasking you, his one and only, with validating his sense of himself as a man. And like it or not, the greatest form of validation is sex. You can take his jacket when he offers it, bake his favorite pie, and fawn over his ability to kill the spider in the bathroom, but if you're not that interested in sex, you're not validating his masculinity.

Denying your partner sex, over time, will register as rejection and ultimately have an impact on his sense of himself as a man. When a guy becomes exclusive with one woman, he's placing her at the center of his sexual universe. She's IT. When she says no over and over again, it takes a toll on his self-esteem; the one person he relies on to make him feel desired and like a man is rejecting him. Or that's how it feels to him.

If a man experiences too much sexual rejection in a relationship, one of three things usually happens:

1. He becomes numb.
    Some guys attempt to deny the rejection by pretending to themselves that they don't really need sex. This never works in the long run. It just leaves them frustrated and resentful.

2. He can keep pestering you.
    Some guys just keep at it, lobbying for sex every chance they get, even though their partners are either denying them outright or giving in begrudgingly. In short order they lose respect for themselves, as do their partners.

3. He can go elsewhere.
    One of the basic reasons a man cheats is a feeling of sexual insecurity and a need to validate himself as a man (this isn't an excuse for infidelity, but it is one of the main causes). A man who feels desperate and resentful will often try to validate himself by seeking out intimacy in other places.

This isn't to say that because your guy's ego might get bruised, he gets to have sex every time he wants it and you have no say in the matter. My point is that refusing him, especially repeatedly, has consequences you may not have considered. No, your guy doesn't get to run your sex life, but it's good for you to understand how to refuse him in a positive way.

Just because a guy is open for business twenty-four hours a day, that doesn't mean you are. You don't have to drop everything and leap into bed whenever he starts getting that look, nor should you feel guilty about it. However, it is good to learn how to say no in a graceful way that communicates delay, not denial.

When you tell your guy no, it's crucial that he's able to accept your refusal while still feeling that you desire him sexually.

Let's say it's a Sunday afternoon, you're working on your laptop trying to make a deadline, and suddenly your partner comes up behind you and starts nuzzling your neck, suggesting you take a break. You know what he wants, but you also need to get this piece of work finished. How do you get on with what you have to do without making him feel sexually inadequate?

Say something like, "Look, I really have to get this done for tomorrow, but I'm going to come and jump you as soon as I get this done, okay?" The tone you're going for here is playful but firm.

This line works for several reasons. First, you have a specific, concise reason for saying no. You're not tossing off some generic, not-in-the-mood reason. Even "Not now, I'm working," can sound like a brush-off. Of course he can *see* you're busy, but that's not what his brain registers. His brain registers: she doesn't desire me, she's making excuses. This may sound like nitpicking, but it's important to understand. When people talk about the fragile male ego, this is what they're talking about.

Logically, he knows that just because you don't want to have sex this very minute, that doesn't mean you've lost all sexual desire for him, but emotionally it feels like a rejection. You know that the only reason you don't want to have sex is that you're swamped with work, but communication is the bedrock of relationships, and what he hears you communicating is: "I don't feel any physical desire for you right now."

For a guy, feeling this kind of rejection from a woman he loves can be excruciating. When a man is single, he can be sexually validated in all sorts of ways: he can go out and flirt and get phone numbers, he can sleep with different women, he can go on three dates a week. But if he is in a monogamous relationship, all of his options for validation rest with you. When he feels that being physical with him isn't that important to you, it begins to dampen his desire, and in the long run, his attraction to you.

One of the keys to a great sex life is to let him know that he's desired. Desirable women receive compliments all the time, but men aren't used to being complimented on their looks and sexuality. A simple comment like "I sort of like it when you don't shave and have a scruffy beard" not only makes your guy feel great about himself, it also increases his attraction for and attachment to you. It takes so little effort to let your guy know he's appreciated in this way, and the reward is that he's completely validated and thus, happy.

Keys to a Great Sex Life

There's an old piece of relationship wisdom that says when sex is good, it's 20 percent of the relationship; when sex is bad, it's 80 percent of the relationship.

Sex is obviously only one component of a great relationship, but it's the cornerstone, so we have to get it right. When it's wrong, it poisons every other part of the relationship. Fortunately, most of the time, as far as the guy is concerned, as long as you're having it regularly he's pretty nonjudgmental. This is one of those rare arenas in where you do get points for trying.

Body confidence

The basis of good sex is not how *he* feels about your body, it's about how *you* feel about it. Sexual attraction is not a matter of how objectively beautiful you are. I know women have insecurities about their bodies. So do men! You might despair over the state of your butt or your stomach, or think your legs are slightly chubby, or despise that birthmark on your neck. But please, please, please—it's not necessary to share your opinions with your guy. If he's undressing you, he wants to see and enjoy every single part of your body.

It's a common, frustrating scenario: a guy starts undressing a woman for the first time, something that most guys savor, and suddenly she wrestles himself out of his arms and zips around the room, switching off all the lights and closing her laptop for good measure.

Now the guy, who moments ago was convinced this woman was an absolute goddess, who was lost in the moment and completely into her, has been alerted to her massive insecurities.

A man gets excited by the idea of having sex with a woman he desires. But if she doesn't act like a desirable woman, he's going to find himself less turned on by the experience. Every time he rubs his hand over your stomach and you move it away to place it on your hip, he notices. He won't understand why you don't find yourself as sexy if he does. He *wants* to see you as the prize, someone he is grateful to have attracted.

When it comes to our imperfections, we have two choices: either do something to change it, or learn to love it.

Most of the time, a man kind of likes the little imperfections. That scar? He actually thought it was kind of cute and wanted to kiss it. Those hips you're worried could be thinner? He likes the way they feel in his hands. That stomach you want to cover up? He likes stroking it.

One thing you can count on—if a guy is sleeping with you, he has already decided he finds you sexy.

Sexual confidence

Sexual confidence is not the same as sexual experience. It's not about knowing everything; it's about the willingness to enjoy sex enough to experiment, to throw yourself into it and learn what you like. The quality of any sexual relationship is defined by the extent to which both people can let themselves go. But again, most guys will be thrilled with the fact that you've made sex a priority.

Variety

In an earlier section I described the vision most guys have for the way their lives should unfold. There is often a time, usually in early adulthood, when a guy is counting on being single, free, and having lots of wild sex with as many women as possible. Regardless of whether a guy ever fulfills this fantasy, the desire for it is based on his male need for variety.

A man who loves his partner and his relationship doesn't possess a lesser need for sexual variety than a player. The only difference is that a player fills his need for variety by sleeping with different women, while the man in a relationship, who has consciously relinquished that requirement, fulfills his need by exploring his appetite and trying new things with his partner.

The guy who's happy in his relationship feels like he gets to have sexual experiences he could never have had when he was single. This is what he must believe in order to feel content being monogamous, especially over time. The way you can ensure he feels that is by showing him that the more he commits to you, the more fun, playful, wild, and exciting things are going to become sexually.

A man in a relationship who is getting his sexual needs fulfilled and feels like he can do those things he fantasizes about is living the dream of most guys. And what's more, it's nearly impossible to act out a lot of these fantasies in the single life. When a guy has a one-night stand with a girl, he's not going to open up to her about all the crazy stuff that he's always wanted to do in the bedroom. He's not going to ask her to try that unusual position, or request that she use her silk scarf to bind his hands. That's the kind of thing he can only bring up in an environment in which he feels safe and he's not going to be judged.

Openness and honesty

In order to have a varied sex life, it's crucial to be open and honest. Men and women both are usually more kinky than anyone who knows them casually would ever assume. We tend to presume that we're the only ones who are turned on by offbeat things, but I guarantee that everyone has a side that they long to bring out with someone who won't judge them, someone who will make them feel comfortable about it. And if a man feels he is in that kind of re-lationship, it's a huge plus for him. When a woman understands and encourages his sexual needs, it is unbelievably powerful. A guy rarely maintains a fantasy element of sleeping with loads of other women when he has a woman at home who's willing to create a sexual world of their own.

The ability to play

Sex is not a final exam. Sex is not estate planning or doing your income taxes. The bedroom should be a place where two people can play in complete comfort, where the two of you can giggle and mess around. The willingness to make sex fun takes the pressure off for him too. The more he feels the environment in your bedroom is both accepting and a little playful, the more likely he is going to be able to relax and please you.

One Rule About Sex

As you know by now, I prefer principles to rules. But I do allow one rule for sex: between the two of you, anything goes.

You may have no interest in indulging a particular fantasy. You may be embarrassed, shocked, or just plain turned off. But it's crucial to adopt an attitude of never say never. Make it your policy to try anything once. (Within reason, of course. If someone suggests something outrageously offensive to you or abusive, run far, run fast. Chances are good he's not the right man for you. You'll know it when you hear it.)

Okay, now that we've mentioned the caveat of keeping yourself safe, here's why you want to consider his fantasy: if your guy mentions there's something he wants to try and you respond by saying, "I would never, ever do that in a million years," an alarm goes off in his head. He may not even feel that invested in whatever it is he's suggesting, but your flat refusal will trigger in him that familiar feeling of panic guys experience when they feel trapped, and when they feel as if a relationship is going to deny them experiences they might have had otherwise.

This, at the end of the day, is why men are terrified of marriage and monogamy. Your refusal to even consider something he might want to try induces one of his worst nightmares, which is a lifetime of unfulfilled sexual needs.

It might sound unreasonable and melodramatic that your categorical refusal to dress up as Princess Leia in her metal bikini can induce such terror, but it's the way his brain is wired. If the door slams on variety, how does he know that it's not also going to shut on everything he wants out of his sex life?

So how do you respond if he wants to do something you don't?

I'll let you in on a secret: men rarely actually do all the crazy stuff that's in their heads. They just want to know that it's not an option closed off to them. Much of the time, they are actually content with just being able to talk about all the stuff they might like to do with you. For most guys, that's enough. So never be afraid of talking about it. Just letting him talk dirty is often enough.

Frequency Matters

There are different kinds of sex, especially in a long-term relationship. It's not going to be mind-blowing all the time, nor, really, does anyone expect it to be. Sometimes he's going to want to have a quickie. Sometimes you're going to want to have a quickie. Sometimes you might be indifferent to the thought of sex, but you know you can be seduced. Sometimes he's just flown in from a business trip and you want to jump his bones, even though he's half asleep. Sometimes you're getting over a cold, or he's stressed at work, and the sex isn't even that hot, but you knock it out anyway. It's all okay. The point is that you're having it. Frequency of sex in a relationship will always matter—though the tally will vary from couple to couple.

Sometimes sex is used merely as a release. All sexual adults sometimes need to address a sexual urge that might not necessarily include his or her partner. To understand and accept this is to accept a basic human impulse. So the next time you are not in the mood for sex, and your guy is aching for it, let him know that you are fine with him taking matters into his own hands, so to speak. You don't want to deny his need, but you don't want to feel like a blow-up doll, either. The solution is simple: masturbation is an option and is not to be judged by either of you. And if you feel inclined to help out, that's okay, too.

All that being said, we know that there are plenty of sexually exciting relationships that fail miserably, and also decades-long relationships where the sexual component may be less important. Even when you get sex right, there are a host of other things that determine whether you keep the guy. As someone wise once said, man cannot live on sex alone. Still, one hard and fast rule to give you an edge to keep the guy: never stop having sex with him.

21

―――

If You Want Him to Commit

In the first part of this book, we discussed the importance of your being a woman of high value. Extraordinary attracts extraordinary, we said.

It also *keeps* extraordinary.

A high-value woman who is also able to embody the traits a guy seeks in a partner—validates him sexually, recognizes his uniqueness, is a loyal teammate, and nurtures and supports him while permitting him to provide and protect—doesn't need to make a case for her desirability. Any guy worth having will realize you are a woman like no other, and he'll sell *himself* on the idea of commitment. As we discussed earlier, a guy must come around to this decision on his own.

What goes on inside a guy's mind when he desires a relationship? First, he needs to feel that life with you is going to get better and better the more he puts into it. Every stage of commitment feels better, richer, and more satisfying than the last phase, because at every step along the way he's earning your investment in him. He believes that the more time and energy he invests in the relationship, the better things are going to get. He comes to associate more pleasure with connection and commitment, because the more he commits, the better

226

things get both emotionally and sexually, and the more available you become to him.

In other words, it should be he who is wondering whether *you* want a relationship with him. Attraction is about keeping him a little off balance. He wants to know you're into him, but he wants to be guessing about whether you want a relationship with him or not. Let him be guessing whether you're seeing other people. He shouldn't know everything up front.

A guy might be in the market for a relationship, but he might not have realized it yet. He's probably not walking around thinking, Yes, that's it, my life would be so much better if I were in a relationship! But then he finds himself hooked on a woman he's been seeing, one he suddenly views as irreplaceable. He realizes that he couldn't have as much fun or as many great experiences with any other woman.

This is why maintaining your fun, exciting lifestyle means everything. And why, moving forward as a couple, it's important to explore new things together. The more you experience together, the more you associate the best adventures of life with one another. It bears mentioning again that we have come full circle. The very qualities that attracted the guy to you in the first place will be the same qualities that get him to commit. It's only a matter of depth.

Don't Skimp on Your Own Value

When you first began dating, your guy was unsure where he stood with you. During this time, you were assessing him to see whether he was worthy of a relationship with you. You were encouraging and playful, flirty and fun, all while getting to know him and learning about his values and standards for those values; at the same time, you were also conveying to him that you weren't desperate to snag a guy, to get into a relationship with just anyone. He may have felt frustrated that things didn't move along quicker, that you weren't willing to sleep with him on the first or second (or tenth) date, but he was impressed that you didn't need to rely on being part of a couple to feel emotionally validated. You were happy with your life and with who you are, and that was enormously attractive to him. He was eager to feel that there was room for him, that he could be part of your fun and varied lifestyle.

Being high value isn't a short-term game we play to attract a guy. The principles for being a high-value woman are relevant in the first ten minutes, or on the tenth date, or after ten years of a relationship.

Your Time Is Still Your Own

It's a common story. A woman is really into a man and she starts giving away too much too soon. She puts herself at his beck and call, dropping friends and work commitments to make him her top priority. We addressed this in the previous section when we talked about premature obligation, but the tenets hold true for this stage of your relationship as well. You don't ever want to put your calendar in his hands and say, "Now that we're dating, here's my schedule. When do you want me?"

In any committed relationship your man will eventually become one of the top priorities in your life, if not the very top. But this position has to be earned. If you hand him your schedule too early, if you put all of your plans on hold and make yourself instantly available to him regardless of what else is going on in your life, it won't endear him to you. Rather, it will compromise the long-term potential of your relationship. I can't say this enough times: a guy should receive the amount of time and attention he earns.

I remember once sending a text to a girl I'd been seeing, asking whether she was free to go out that evening. She sent back this message: "That would be great. But I'm fully booked in the evenings this week, big piece of work due so I have a date with my desk. How about we do lunch instead?"

I liked this message because it established the principles we have talked about here. On one hand she expressed a desire to see me. On the other, she made it clear that because I was relatively new to her life I wasn't as important as her work at this stage, so I'd have to wait my turn. She expressed her high value by showing that she wasn't compromising on important things just because a guy asked her out, and so she became that much more attractive to me.

When you realize a guy you like feels the same about you, clinging to his attraction for dear life in the hope of maintaining it never works. It doesn't make him more attracted and more interested in committing to you, but less. Bending over backward to be available to him merely shows him that you're not as high value as he once imagined. Indeed, the more you mold your personality to become what he says he likes, the less respect he has for you over time. Remember that amazing, high-value woman he gathered up his courage to ask on that first date? That's the woman he still wants.

Here's an image that some of the women I've coached have found helpful:

Think of your life as a train that's pulling in for a short stop at the station. It stops to pick up new passengers, but the many exciting destinations ahead require the train to keep moving; it can't afford to stop for long.

Your guy is standing on the platform as the train pulls in. He has plenty of time to climb aboard. He already has the itinerary; he knows where the train is going, what route it's going to take, and where it will stop along the way.

He also knows that the train will be leaving the platform shortly. It will not wait around for him to get on board. He'll have a great journey if he decides to climb aboard, but the itinerary hasn't been designed with him in mind. The decision to come along or not is his, but the train isn't going to sit in the station, waiting for him to make it.

If he decides to stay put, fine, but he needs to stand back behind the yellow line, because this train is leaving the station and may not come back around again. All aboard!

Tend to Your Lifestyle

As close and connected as you may feel to your new guy, he should never have the sense that he's going about his business while you're sitting at home waiting for him to call. This is why tending to your lifestyle is so important to keeping a guy long term. The same lifestyle you were building for your own pleasure should remain as valuable to you as it was before he came along. And you should continue to build it. Even though you may now define yourself as part of a couple, you still need to keep giving him little glimpses into how fun and exciting life can be with you.

Let's return for a moment to the train metaphor. You're going to give him a chance to get on board if he wants to, but he's going to have to be quick about it, because you have places to go. If, on the other hand, you don't have anywhere else to be, and you just stop at his platform and say, "Okay, take your time. I'll just be waiting here whenever you're in the mood to hop on the train," a guy immediately feels a lack of urgency. He knows that whatever he does, no matter how long he keeps you waiting, you're not going to leave without him, so he has no incentive to get on board now. If he knows you'll be there all day and all week, he can put off his decision indefinitely.

Maintain Your Standards

Although it's tempting to compromise your standards in the early months of dating in the belief that being agreeable and frictionless will keep the connection moving forward, it's crucial to stick to your guns. Uphold the same standards you displayed when you first met. Men adhere to the parameters women set for them, and a woman with standards gives a guy something to live up to.

This never changes, no matter how long you are together.

What gets confusing for guys is the degree to which you lower your standards at the beginning of a relationship, only to raise them a few months later. For example, if his continual texting while you're out on a date annoys you, you might refrain from telling him you don't like it because you don't want to seem disagreeable or demanding, for fear of losing him. But this sets you up for disaster later on. If, six months down the road, you try to bring up the fact that it annoys you, he's going to wonder why you're suddenly mad about it if you never said so before. Continuing to live by your standards shows your guy that he isn't going to win you over just because you've been dating for a few months. It gives him the sense that until you're committed to him—and in some ways, ever after—you're still scoping him out, which gives him the chance to position himself as someone worthy of being important to you.

I'm not advocating game playing; this is about valuing yourself enough to know that you're entitled to a certain quality of person with whom to share your life. True power is knowing in the deepest part of yourself that you always have the ability to walk away. If he's wrong for you, you know there are thousands more guys out there.

Don't give him all the benefits of a relationship before he has committed to one

When it comes to love, men and women tend to run on different time-tables. Three months into the relationship she's starting to wonder whether they might one day get engaged, while he's still thinking they're just hanging out. She chose him weeks earlier, and he's start-ing to think the time has come for him to think about choosing. This is why it's important to let things develop organically. You may be moving *toward* a relationship with your guy, but if you're not in one yet, don't jump the gun and rush into relationship mode. In the same way that the number of dates doesn't determine when you decide to have sex with someone, there's no time limit after which your time to-gether accrues and you're suddenly in a Relationship. Even if it's going extremely well, one has to allow it to unfold naturally. Never simply assume you're exclusive.

Rushing the relationship is counterproductive for several reasons. The guy may panic because he feels things are moving too quickly. He won't appreciate what he's got because he hasn't done anything to get it and will also have no incentive to invest more, because why should he?

Recall the principle of reciprocity discussed in chapter 6: give first, expect second. Invest first, then see how he responds. A guy should only receive based on the amount that he invests. And you should always act based on how much he invests, not on how much you like him.

If you overinvest, giving your guy all the benefits of a relationship immediately—arranging your schedule around his, giving yourself emotionally to him regardless of whether he shows the same affection and openness toward you—then he isn't going to appreciate it, or you. Men only appreciate what they've earned.

This concept is not only applicable to men. Look at it from an-other angle: Suppose a guy bought you a car after one date. Nice as that might sound, if it actually happened you wouldn't feel impressed and appreciative; you'd feel weird and suspicious that he was trying to buy your affection. Even if you loved it, you'd reject the gift as inappropriate. You may have had a great time on your date, but you hardly know the guy.

When a guy gets all your time, devotion, and sexual attention before he's ready, it feels awkward, not wonderful. He may have been hoping to one day be a big part of your life, but he needs to feel like he's earned it; otherwise he's going to reject it. We've mentioned this before, but it's worth repeating here. It's another facet of a guy's basic insecurity: he needs to feel as if only he could have won you. He doesn't want to feel as if just any guy who took you out for enough cheeseburgers and movies could have landed you.

How can you tell if he's investing in you and your relationship? Ask yourself: Is he setting aside time for you? Does he make an effort to bring you into his daily life on a regular basis? Is he confiding in you? Does he enjoy doing simple workaday things together, or is he just interested in getting together at 10 p.m.? He may not be racing to introduce you to his mother the moment you become an item, but he should be showing increasing amounts of investment by bringing you into his life more and more. These are the things you should be looking for, and adjust your investment accordingly.

I'm not saying you shouldn't be affectionate. I'm also not suggesting that you should bust his chops for the aforementioned 10 p.m. phone call.

Let's talk about that phone call for a moment. The longer you're with someone, the less like a booty call it becomes and the more like something we don't have a name for. Maybe the French do. It's a gray area. You're in a kind-of-committed relationship with this guy, so don't you owe it to him to make an exception and tell him to come on over?

Well, no, actually. He knows that it's too late to be calling, but he's hoping you might like him so much you're willing to overinvest and say yes. Maybe you'll say yes because you're afraid that saying no will cause him to lose interest, or to call someone else in his phonebook. Your response is going to give him information about how much he can get without having to return the investment.

In the immediate moment it might seem hot and sexy, but the next morning a subtle shift may have occurred in your dynamic: now he's seen that you are willing to compromise your standards just because you like him. And if he hasn't already committed to any kind of relationship, you've now just sent the message that it doesn't matter whether he does, because he's still going to get all the benefits of being in a relationship without having to actually be in one.

If you are seeing a guy and you get one of those late-night phone calls, as you most certainly will, you don't have to reject him in a serious way.

Tell him you're already in your PJs, or that it's too short notice for you and you've got plans to be asleep at the moment. This lightness of tone shows that you may not be interested, but you're not angry. You're not punishing him for asking, only showing him that you can't be cajoled into giving him his way that easily.

Assess and invest on what you see, not what you hope for

Another reason we sometimes overinvest is because we're in love with someone's potential. If I was forced to choose one dating scenario that never leads to happiness, it's investing in a guy who's a fixer-upper, who isn't great relationship material now but might be sometime in the unforeseeable future.

An acquaintance of mine met a guy with whom she fell head over heels. On their first date he talked with great passion about wanting to spend the next five years traveling around the world, after which he might think about settling down. My friend didn't think he was going to be able to get the money together to take that sort of extended trip, but she began overinvesting like mad, and things fell apart quickly.

Her mistake was in not believing him. He might not have been going around the block, but he also wasn't giving her a single sign that he was interested in investing in a relationship with her. This is what happens when we fall for someone's potential instead of the person in front of us.

PUTTING YOUR FOOT DOWN

I show you why you shouldn't stand for shoddy behavior and how to communicate your demands in a way that remains high value.

Go to **www.gettheguybook.com/standards**
Access code: **gtgbook**

Flip the Script:
Changing His Perception of Commitment

Often you'll date a guy for a few weeks, and then the awkward moment arises when he calls you—or, if he's more courageous than most of us, asks to see you—to deliver the news that he's not really looking for anything serious. Who knows why he's saying this. Maybe he's just been through a bad breakup, or maybe he's just scared. The reasons don't matter. The only thing that matters is how you respond to the situation.

I was this guy, not long ago. I had just crawled out of a painful relationship. I felt exhausted and raw. I told myself I wasn't going to get serious with anyone again for a long time. There was not a guy in the known world who wanted a relationship less than I did. Then, unexpectedly, I met someone new who I really liked. We went on some dates. We really connected, things were going well, and I realized that we were beginning to get close. I freaked out. I started to panic.

I didn't want a relationship. As much as I genuinely liked this woman, relationships spelled responsibility, pain, drama, emotional exhaustion—all the things I was desperate to avoid. I kept telling myself that I had to put a stop to this.

One day, after another great date, I drove her back to her place, parked, switched off the ignition, slowly turned to her, and said, "Listen . . ." I had broken into a sweat. I couldn't believe I was about to dump the old cliché into the lap of someone I liked so much: "I don't want anything serious right now. I mean, I'm not looking for a relationship."

I braced myself for her response. I expected rage, tears, or at least annoyance. Maybe some sharp sarcasm. I expected her to tell me that if that was the case she never wanted to see me again. But she did none of those things.

"Okay," she said, and then playfully added, "I'm not asking you to marry me, you know."

I was taken aback. All I could say was, "Okay. Cool."

"Cool," she said. She gave me an extremely sexy kiss, smiled, went in the house, and that was that.

But for me, that wasn't that.

As I was driving home I started feeling like an idiot. Why did I say that? I thought. Why did I bother bringing that up? Why did I get so dramatic all of a sudden? Now I felt like the one who was taking shit too seriously. She didn't seem effected by my proclamation one way or the other. Because she didn't take it seriously and reacted unemotionally, it defused all my seriousness. We were, indeed, cool.

I wanted to see her again. A few days later I asked her to

come over on Friday for dinner. She didn't mention our conversation, just said, "I'm out with friends on Friday, maybe Sunday afternoon?"

"That's fine," I said. But it wasn't fine. Now she was dictating things *on her terms.* When Sunday arrived I expected her to be a bit frosty or withholding, but she was as fun and sexy as ever; she was incredible, and we had an amazing time. But then she left. I thought, Man, I have so much fun with this girl. So I tried to see her again two days later. She said, "I've got a lot of work this week, how about Saturday?" And I thought, That's five days away, I want to see her now! Why do I have to wait this long?

After a couple of weeks I brought up the commitment conversation again. This time, I wanted to make sure I got it right. "Listen," I said, "about what I said before. I don't know why I said all that stuff. I was being stupid. I really do want a relationship with you."

She smiled and said, "Okay, great. Are you sure?"

"Yes!" I said. "Of course I'm sure."

And I was.

Let's look at how she flipped the script on me:

1. When I said I didn't want commitment, she accepted it calmly.

Had she yelled or cried, I would have been able to say to myself, "Look how crazy she's acting, no wonder I don't want a relationship with her." Instead, I was left alone with my actions.

When I was growing up, my brothers and I were always well behaved. We didn't disobey our parents or take drugs or run away, or do any of those rebellious things most kids do. I said to my dad some years later, "You had three teenage boys and not one of us turned out to be a loose cannon. Why do you think that was?" He gave a nonchalant shrug and said, "I never gave you anything to rebel against."

That's what this woman did. She may have been upset, but in keeping it to herself she deprived me of something to rebel against. Most guys are like kids; when they test the boundaries and see that nothing happens, they feel no need to aggressively assert their independence. As I said before, some guys just need time to sell themselves on the idea. Sometimes a guy will say he doesn't want commitment simply because that's his default setting. Rather than getting angry or otherwise reacting strongly, show that it's not a big deal to you (this is why it's so important to have a lifestyle that makes you feel like you have the ability to create options; instead of faking being in demand, you have to actually be in demand).

2. The moment I said I wasn't interested in a relationship, she placed me at the bottom of her list of priorities.

Even though she liked me, once I told her I didn't want anything serious, *she made me less of a priority.* She showed me that she was fine being casual, but that she was then going to treat things a bit more casually. She was only giving me what I was willing to invest. So instead of giving me the benefits of a relationship, now I was made (with good reason) less important than all her other commitments—friends, family, work, hobbies, her free time.

3. She still brought her best self to the table.

Even though I had been relegated to a lower place on her priority list, she still brought her best self every time I saw her. Even though I said I'd wanted to be casual, she was just as much fun as she'd ever been. She was still sexy and flirty, we still were affectionate and intimate. Everything was as wonderful as it had been before, but I got less of it, because I got less of her.

Even though I was the one who'd told her I wasn't interested in a serious relationship, she was going to do things on her terms. I told her I wanted to be casual and she accepted my wishes. But she wasn't about to give me the benefits of being in a relationship with her. She showed me in no uncertain terms that her train wasn't going to stop moving and wait for me to get on it. Instead, she used her actions to let me sell me on the idea of commitment, which I couldn't do quickly enough.

22

Love for Life

During the course of writing this book, I received a call from *Cosmopolitan* UK, asking me to speak at a bridal seminar they were sponsoring at a fancy hotel in London. I was thrilled to be invited. Even though my reputation has been built on getting the guy, it seemed that the people at *Cosmo* thought I could share some wisdom with a group of brides-to-be. I welcomed the opportunity, especially because it confirmed my feeling that what I teach is relevant to all stages of relationships, from first conversation to fiftieth wedding anniversary. In contrast to the audience at most of my seminars, women who consider themselves unlucky in love (and whose attitudes aren't always easy to turn toward optimism), these *Cosmo* readers would be on top of the world. Now that they had found love, surely they would be open, willing, and eager to pick up some tips about how to make the most of their marriage.

Ten minutes into my talk, I realized I couldn't have been more wrong. In fact, this crowd was going to be the most challenging one ever. What could I possibly tell them that they didn't already know? These women were giddy with success, flush with the certainty that their lifelong dream of finding their guy had been fulfilled. My advice was valuable only for those other women who, poor souls, can't find their rightful mates. Save it for the singles, they seemed to say.

And who could blame them? What could be better than the moment when a couple makes ritual vows to each other for life? The rest is easy. Right?

I congratulated them on their upcoming nuptials, but did my best to send them away with some useful advice.

Marriage is the beginning of something beautiful. But to keep it beautiful, the courtship must never end. Though that courtship will change as long-term familiarity and depth of love grow from shared experience, the tenets of maintaining high standards and holding tight to your high-value qualities will always apply. Sticking to these deeply held beliefs will have everything to do with the success of the marriage.

"If you take anything away with you from this talk today," I told my impatient listeners, "please let it be this: don't let complacency creep between you and your husband and threaten the foundation you built together. And, whatever you do . . . never, ever, *ever* stop having sex with him."

They laughed at that last line, but I hoped that months or years or decades down the line, what I was saying would ring true. Getting the guy to marry you is just the beginning.

═══

Of the many women I've coached throughout the years, while some are twenty-one-year-olds on their own for the first time searching for Mr. Right, just as many come from a spectrum of experiences. I've helped women in their thirties who have enjoyed dating for years and who now want to get serious. There are women in their forties who've been married and divorced, and are ready to try again. And there are women in their fifties and sixties, stunned to find themselves widows, who still hope to find again someone with whom to share their lives. As I said in the beginning of this book, one of the amazing things about love is that regardless what happens to us in life, most of us yearn to try again.

One of the most often asked questions at events or seminars, or even in conversation, is "Will this work for someone my age?" I tell them what I've learned to be true: "You're never too old to be youthful."

Whenever I hear someone trot out that old adage "Youth is wasted on the young," I tell them, "Actually, youth is wasted on everybody."

I don't possess the wisdom of old age, but I'm smart enough to have listened to and learned from people that do. Youthfulness has no age limit. Our concept of age is relative. I know people in their nineties who have more spirit and fervor than a lot of people in their twenties. People in their forties are nostalgic for their youthful thirties, and people in their seventies think they were young in their fifties. You think you're young? You'll soon be old. And if you think you're old, you'll soon be older.

There will come a day, perhaps not far in the future, when you will look at pictures of yourself at the age you are now, and you'll be shocked at how young and beautiful you were. Perhaps you will be amazed that you spent any time at all focusing on your perceived flaws and failings instead of pursuing the things you wanted. You will see a person who had all of her life ahead of her, a woman with so many possibilities, so many opportunities and choices. Take advantage of them now.

My oldest client was a woman who followed my online program at home. She e-mailed me to say, "I want you to pass on a message to everyone you coach. I'm 83 years old and I'm retired. Through your coaching I've met the man of my dreams. We're spending our days right now building a boat, and when it's done, we're going to sail away in it together. If it can happen to me at my age, with everything I've been through in my life, it can happen to anyone."

======

Love is one of the greatest sources of happiness in the world. If you follow the lessons set out in this book you'll get your guy. But life isn't just about love, and regardless of how your own story plays out, there will never be a time when what I've posited here won't serve you. All the lessons here may be directed at getting the guy, but they are, at bottom, about getting a life that matters to you.

Learning and practicing the art of creating rather than waiting; throwing the net wide in order to meet a lot of people, men and women alike, who will enrich your life; operating from a mindset of abundance, not scarcity; developing and adhering to the attributes of a woman of high value; upholding your own standards; understanding that you are in control of your own choices—these skills strengthen your sense of self-worth and will improve all areas of your life. It's the project of a lifetime. Your love life will get better, but so will your mood and attitude, your performance on the job, your friendships, and your ability to set and achieve personal goals.

If I could distill the wisdom set forth here into a simple message, it would be this: believe in your own value and every good thing in life will follow.

GO FORTH AND FIND LOVE

I'm not willing to let you go yet. Join me for a proper send-off.

Go to **www.gettheguybook.com/congratulations**
Access code: **gtgbook**

Acknowledgments

The greatest gift of my life has been the self-confidence instilled by so many who have believed in me. There are many more than I can list here, but I've done my best to name a few.

Family first: My parents, who told me I was great long before there was any legitimate reason to do so. My dad, Steve, who taught me what it was to take risks and never stop trying, and my mum, Pauline, the master of empathy and sensitivity. Both skill sets have been equally important in my getting here today. They will always be my best friends in the world.

My youngest brother, Harry, whose pride in me means more than he knows, and whose effortless genius will always amaze me.

My middle brother, Stephen, who worked tirelessly to cowrite this book with me and treated it as if it were his own. An immensely talented writer who did me an enormous favor by being with me till the end.

Edward Whitehead, my right-hand man, without whom I would be lost. A young and disgustingly bright colleague and friend for whom I am grateful every single day.

Those who have helped over the years with the content and ideas behind this book: Raphael Dworkin, Sloane Delancer, David Dipper, Kathryn Bilverstone, Adam Lyons, and Michael Roche.

The team at Get The Guy past and present: Raj Khedun, John Ross, Siobhan Robinson (my angel!), Rhen A. Khong, Martin Hetzel,

Monica Millares, Kim Zaninovich, Seema Gulrajani, Lucy Counter, Andrew Baker, Kelvin Ke, John Maguire, Chandima Nethisinghe, Ivana Nemcova, Stephen Costello, Adam Abdulla, Doug Haines, Bie Hernando, Jamela Mundell, and Daiyaan Ghani, all of whom, over the years, in one way or another, helped me reach millions of women worldwide through Get The Guy.

My mentors along the way: Justin Howard, who gave me my first office floor to sleep on. My dad, the person I can go to any time of day for help, advice, and motivation. Richard La Ruina, who gave me the opportunity to shine when nobody knew who I was.

My book agents, Heather Holden-Brown, Elly James at HHB Agency, and Richard Pine at Inkwell Management, all of whom delivered exactly what they promised and more.

My publisher Michelle Signore and her team at Transworld for first believing in this book's potential and being part of my journey.

My publisher and mentor Karen Rinaldi and her team at Harper-Collins, including Jake Zebede, Kate Blum, and Tina Andreadis (the biggest cheerleader I could hope for). Leah Wasielewski, Mark Ferguson, and Katie O'Callaghan for all their help with the marketing of this book.

Karen Karbo, the wonderful and caring writer who came on board to work with me in the late stages of the book. Her nurturing and gentle nature was the perfect complement to my often heavy-handed approach.

The journalists who have written honest and fair reviews of my work over the years, including Alison Tay, Katie Mulloy, and Nicki Bailey.

My dear friends at Creative Visionaries, Jon Turteltaub, Simon Edington, Kathy Eldon, Amy Eldon, Michael Bender, and Catherine Cunningham, who have taken me on a roller-coaster ride through the United States that led to my getting a show on NBC.

Everyone who has made my TV career possible: Sean Perry and Ivo Fischer at WME, David Garfinkle and Jay Renfroe at Renegade

Productions, Virginia Hill at Gogglebox Entertainment, Jason Ehrlich, Peter Higgins, Susan House, Greg Goldman, Louise Roe, Philomena Muinzer, Bill and Giuliana Rancic, Eva Longoria, Camilo Valdes, and Sloane Delancer.

My favorite schoolteachers, Mr. Dunn and Mr. Haskett, who taught me what it is to teach with heart.

As important as anyone on this list, my clients over the years, many of whom are now dear friends. You have all taught me so much about life and human nature. Without you none of this would have been possible.

Lastly, the friends and family along the way: Billy, Kasey, Danny, Sam, Shirley, Uncle Pete, Jamie, Michael Gendi. Thanks to Ollie Powell for making sure I didn't fail university while building my business. And thanks to those who have kept me sane: Ian Austin, Clive Nichol, Rob Unterhalter, Richard Pentecost, Bobby "Bistro" Bull, Will Gilburt, Rory Barker, and all the others who have been there for me along the way. I love you all!

About the Author

Matthew Hussey is an international speaker and human dynamics coach. He is the star of NBC's *Ready for Love* and a regular expert on MTV's *Plain Jane*.

His live events and online programs have gained international status, with tens of thousands of individuals coming through them every year.

Matthew's live events include intensive love-life coaching weekends, transformative five-day retreats, and programs for individuals looking to increase their personal impact in their private and professional lives.

He is regularly hired for speaking engagements with companies such as Procter & Gamble, Accenture, and Virgin. Matthew has also worked on product launches with Hugo Boss, Bare Escentuals, and the Perfume Shop.

He has been invited to speak in front of British royalty and the students of Oxford University, and he has hosted the Sales Consultant of the Year Awards with Procter & Gamble.

Matthew regularly works with well known individuals, from Christina Aguilera to CEOs and senior directors of Fortune 500 companies.

When not traveling, Matthew divides his time between London and Los Angeles.

You can find him online at www.matthewhussey.com.

See Matthew's live-event calendar:
www.matthewhussey.com/live

See Matthew's online programs:
www.matthewhussey.com/online

Hire Matthew for a speaking engagement:
www.matthewhussey.com/speaking